W. VANCE - J. VAN HAMME

FOR MARIA

XIII

Colour work: PETRA

9th CINEBOOK
The 9th Art Publisher

Original title: Pour Maria

Original edition: © Dargaud Benelux (Dargaud-Lombard SA), 1992
by Van Hamme & Vance
www.dargaud.com
All rights reserved

English translation: © 2011 Cinebook Ltd

Translator: Jerome Saincantin

Lettering and text layout: Imadjinn
Printed in Spain by Just Colour Graphic

This edition first published in Great Britain in 2011 by
Cinebook Ltd
56 Beech Avenue
Canterbury, Kent
CT4 7TA
www.cinebook.com

A CIP catalogue record for this book
is available from the British Library

ISBN 978-1-84918-093-1

9th CINEBOOK
The 9th Art Publisher

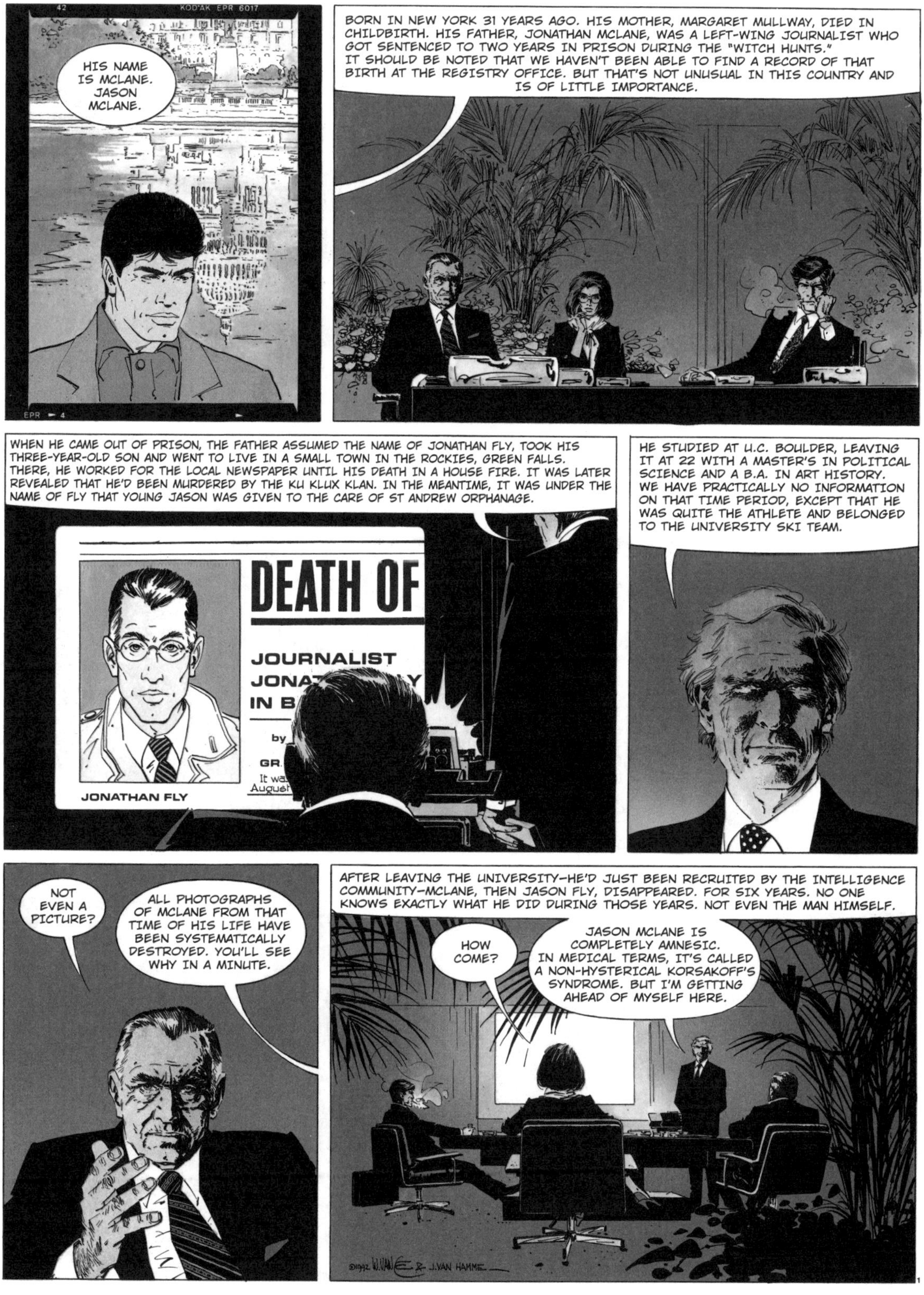
KODAK EPR 6017
HIS NAME IS MCLANE. JASON MCLANE.
BORN IN NEW YORK 31 YEARS AGO. HIS MOTHER, MARGARET MULLWAY, DIED IN CHILDBIRTH. HIS FATHER, JONATHAN MCLANE, WAS A LEFT-WING JOURNALIST WHO GOT SENTENCED TO TWO YEARS IN PRISON DURING THE "WITCH HUNTS." IT SHOULD BE NOTED THAT WE HAVEN'T BEEN ABLE TO FIND A RECORD OF THAT BIRTH AT THE REGISTRY OFFICE. BUT THAT'S NOT UNUSUAL IN THIS COUNTRY AND IS OF LITTLE IMPORTANCE.
WHEN HE CAME OUT OF PRISON, THE FATHER ASSUMED THE NAME OF JONATHAN FLY, TOOK HIS THREE-YEAR-OLD SON AND WENT TO LIVE IN A SMALL TOWN IN THE ROCKIES, GREEN FALLS. THERE, HE WORKED FOR THE LOCAL NEWSPAPER UNTIL HIS DEATH IN A HOUSE FIRE. IT WAS LATER REVEALED THAT HE'D BEEN MURDERED BY THE KU KLUX KLAN. IN THE MEANTIME, IT WAS UNDER THE NAME OF FLY THAT YOUNG JASON WAS GIVEN TO THE CARE OF ST ANDREW ORPHANAGE.
DEATH OF
JOURNALIST
JONATHAN FLY
HE STUDIED AT U.C. BOULDER, LEAVING IT AT 22 WITH A MASTER'S IN POLITICAL SCIENCE AND A B.A. IN ART HISTORY. WE HAVE PRACTICALLY NO INFORMATION ON THAT TIME PERIOD, EXCEPT THAT HE WAS QUITE THE ATHLETE AND BELONGED TO THE UNIVERSITY SKI TEAM.
NOT EVEN A PICTURE?
ALL PHOTOGRAPHS OF MCLANE FROM THAT TIME OF HIS LIFE HAVE BEEN SYSTEMATICALLY DESTROYED. YOU'LL SEE WHY IN A MINUTE.
AFTER LEAVING THE UNIVERSITY—HE'D JUST BEEN RECRUITED BY THE INTELLIGENCE COMMUNITY—MCLANE, THEN JASON FLY, DISAPPEARED. FOR SIX YEARS. NO ONE KNOWS EXACTLY WHAT HE DID DURING THOSE YEARS. NOT EVEN THE MAN HIMSELF.
HOW COME?
JASON MCLANE IS COMPLETELY AMNESIC. IN MEDICAL TERMS, IT'S CALLED A NON-HYSTERICAL KORSAKOFF'S SYNDROME. BUT I'M GETTING AHEAD OF MYSELF HERE.
©1992 W. VANCE & J. VAN HAMME

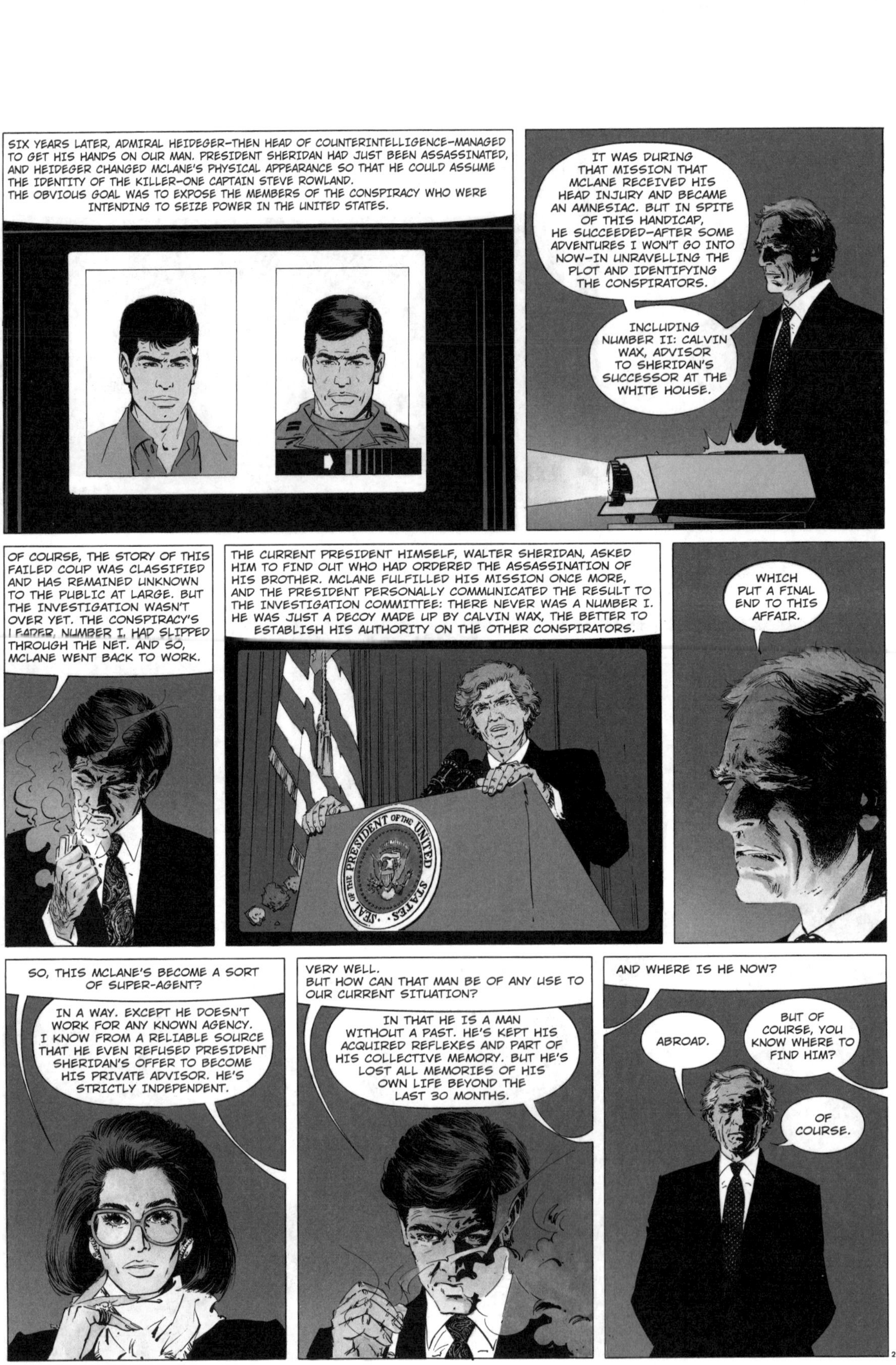

SIX YEARS LATER, ADMIRAL HEIDEGER—THEN HEAD OF COUNTERINTELLIGENCE—MANAGED TO GET HIS HANDS ON OUR MAN. PRESIDENT SHERIDAN HAD JUST BEEN ASSASSINATED, AND HEIDEGER CHANGED MCLANE'S PHYSICAL APPEARANCE SO THAT HE COULD ASSUME THE IDENTITY OF THE KILLER—ONE CAPTAIN STEVE ROWLAND. THE OBVIOUS GOAL WAS TO EXPOSE THE MEMBERS OF THE CONSPIRACY WHO WERE INTENDING TO SEIZE POWER IN THE UNITED STATES.
IT WAS DURING THAT MISSION THAT MCLANE RECEIVED HIS HEAD INJURY AND BECAME AN AMNESIAC. BUT IN SPITE OF THIS HANDICAP, HE SUCCEEDED—AFTER SOME ADVENTURES I WON'T GO INTO NOW—IN UNRAVELLING THE PLOT AND IDENTIFYING THE CONSPIRATORS.
INCLUDING NUMBER II: CALVIN WAX, ADVISOR TO SHERIDAN'S SUCCESSOR AT THE WHITE HOUSE.
OF COURSE, THE STORY OF THIS FAILED COUP WAS CLASSIFIED AND HAS REMAINED UNKNOWN TO THE PUBLIC AT LARGE. BUT THE INVESTIGATION WASN'T OVER YET. THE CONSPIRACY'S LEADER, NUMBER I, HAD SLIPPED THROUGH THE NET. AND SO, MCLANE WENT BACK TO WORK.
THE CURRENT PRESIDENT HIMSELF, WALTER SHERIDAN, ASKED HIM TO FIND OUT WHO HAD ORDERED THE ASSASSINATION OF HIS BROTHER. MCLANE FULFILLED HIS MISSION ONCE MORE, AND THE PRESIDENT PERSONALLY COMMUNICATED THE RESULT TO THE INVESTIGATION COMMITTEE: THERE NEVER WAS A NUMBER I. HE WAS JUST A DECOY MADE UP BY CALVIN WAX, THE BETTER TO ESTABLISH HIS AUTHORITY ON THE OTHER CONSPIRATORS.
SEAL OF THE PRESIDENT OF THE UNITED STATES
WHICH PUT A FINAL END TO THIS AFFAIR.
SO, THIS MCLANE'S BECOME A SORT OF SUPER-AGENT?
IN A WAY. EXCEPT HE DOESN'T WORK FOR ANY KNOWN AGENCY. I KNOW FROM A RELIABLE SOURCE THAT HE EVEN REFUSED PRESIDENT SHERIDAN'S OFFER TO BECOME HIS PRIVATE ADVISOR. HE'S STRICTLY INDEPENDENT.
VERY WELL. BUT HOW CAN THAT MAN BE OF ANY USE TO OUR CURRENT SITUATION?
IN THAT HE IS A MAN WITHOUT A PAST. HE'S KEPT HIS ACQUIRED REFLEXES AND PART OF HIS COLLECTIVE MEMORY. BUT HE'S LOST ALL MEMORIES OF HIS OWN LIFE BEYOND THE LAST 30 MONTHS.
AND WHERE IS HE NOW?
ABROAD.
BUT OF COURSE, YOU KNOW WHERE TO FIND HIM?
OF COURSE.
2

LET'S LOOK AT THE FACTS. AFTER FINISHING COLLEGE, MCLANE DISAPPEARS FOR SIX YEARS. WHEN HE REAPPEARS, HE FIGHTS LIKE A HIGHLY TRAINED PROFESSIONAL, CAN HANDLE JUST ABOUT ANY WEAPON AND SPEAKS FLUENT SPANISH.
LATIN AMERICA, THEN.
MORE THAN LIKELY. AND WHERE IS THE BEST WAR SCHOOL IN ALL OF LATIN AMERICA?
CUBA?
CUBA. THE SECRET TRAINING CENTRE OF THE SIERRA MAESTRA. BACK THEN, IT WAS RUN BY THE BEST SOVIET SPECIALISTS.
SO, WE COULD ASSUME THAT THIS MCLANE WAS TRAINED IN CUBA?
WE COULD, EVEN THOUGH WE CAN'T BE CERTAIN. BUT THE IMPORTANT PART IS THAT MCLANE CAN'T BE CERTAIN EITHER!
NOW, LET'S LOOK AT THIS PICTURE YOU ALL KNOW. THE ONE THAT WAS WIDELY SHOWN IN THE PRESS THREE YEARS AGO. PRECISELY AT THE TIME WHEN MCLANE RESURFACED.
SAME HEIGHT, SAME BUILD, SAME AGE... AND ABOVE ALL, BEFORE HIS DEATH, THE SAME QUALITIES AS A MAN OF ACTION. I'M SURE YOU'LL AGREE THAT SUCH SIMILARITIES ARE ALMOST UNCANNY.
NOW, LADY, GENTLEMEN, DO YOU UNDERSTAND WHY JASON MCLANE IS PRECISELY THE MAN WE NEED?
SAN MIGUEL INTERNATIONAL AIRPORT, A FEW WEEKS LATER...
BWIA International
BWIA
SAN MIGUEL

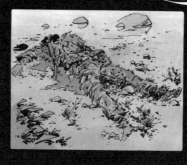

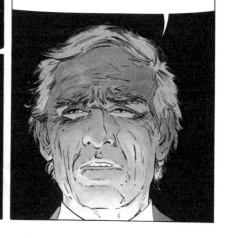

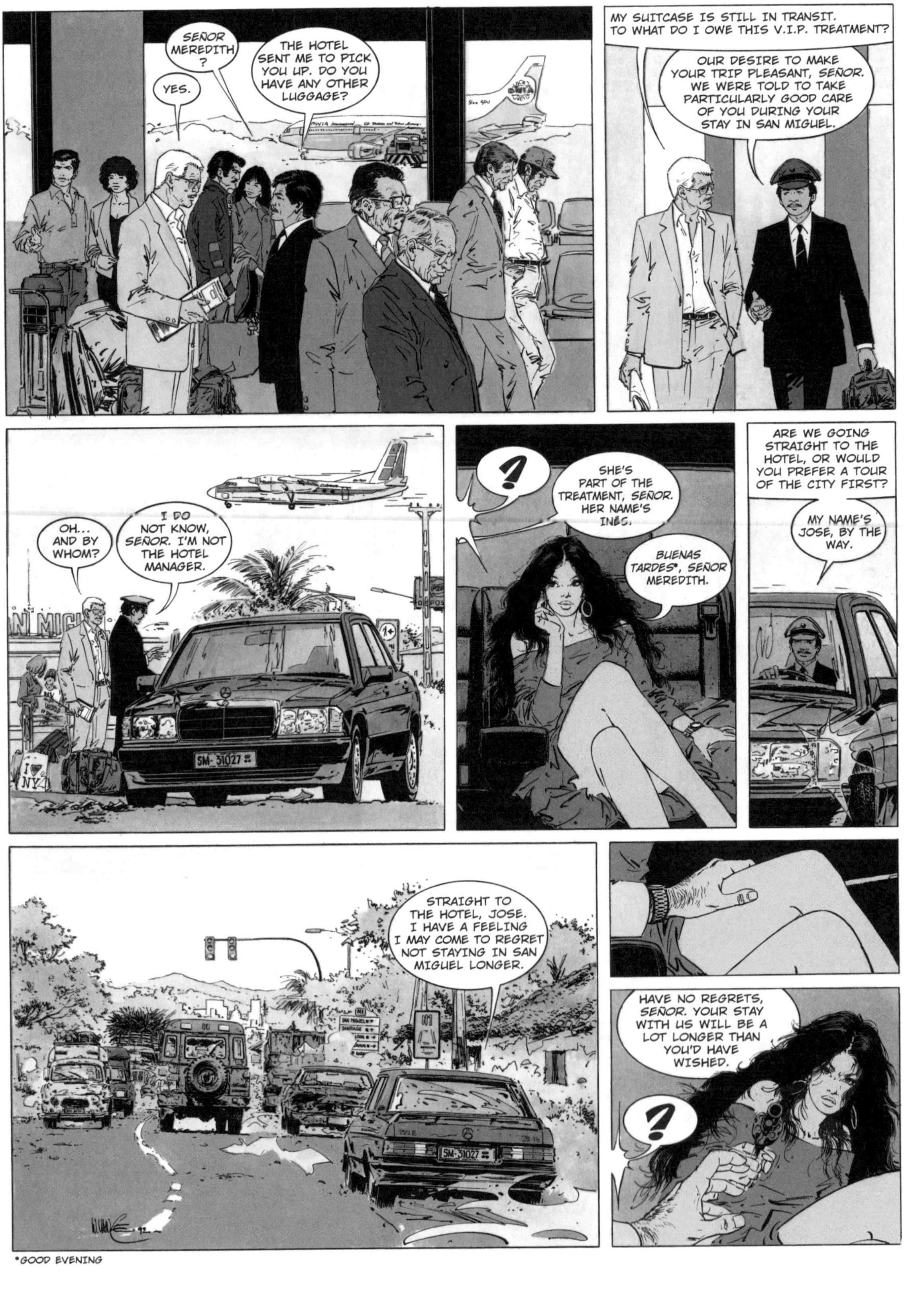
SEÑOR MEREDITH?
YES.
THE HOTEL SENT ME TO PICK YOU UP. DO YOU HAVE ANY OTHER LUGGAGE?
MY SUITCASE IS STILL IN TRANSIT. TO WHAT DO I OWE THIS V.I.P. TREATMENT?
OUR DESIRE TO MAKE YOUR TRIP PLEASANT, SEÑOR. WE WERE TOLD TO TAKE PARTICULARLY GOOD CARE OF YOU DURING YOUR STAY IN SAN MIGUEL.
OH... AND BY WHOM?
I DO NOT KNOW, SEÑOR. I'M NOT THE HOTEL MANAGER.
SM-31027
?
SHE'S PART OF THE TREATMENT, SEÑOR. HER NAME'S INÉS.
BUENAS TARDES*, SEÑOR MEREDITH.
ARE WE GOING STRAIGHT TO THE HOTEL, OR WOULD YOU PREFER A TOUR OF THE CITY FIRST?
MY NAME'S JOSE, BY THE WAY.
STRAIGHT TO THE HOTEL, JOSE. I HAVE A FEELING I MAY COME TO REGRET NOT STAYING IN SAN MIGUEL LONGER.
SM-31027
HAVE NO REGRETS, SEÑOR. YOUR STAY WITH US WILL BE A LOT LONGER THAN YOU'D HAVE WISHED.
?

*GOOD EVENING

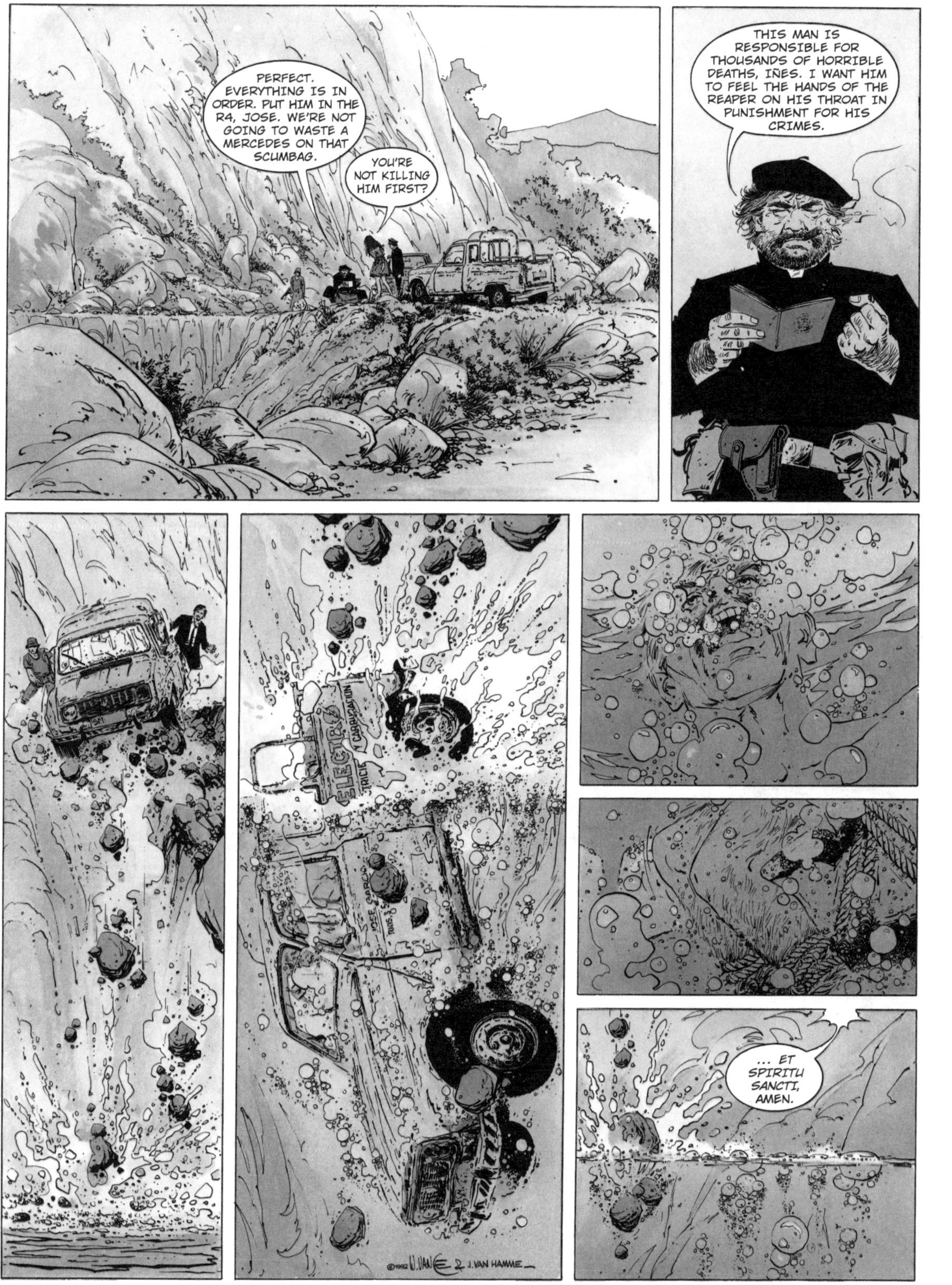
PERFECT. EVERYTHING IS IN ORDER. PUT HIM IN THE R4, JOSE. WE'RE NOT GOING TO WASTE A MERCEDES ON THAT SCUMBAG.
YOU'RE NOT KILLING HIM FIRST?
THIS MAN IS RESPONSIBLE FOR THOUSANDS OF HORRIBLE DEATHS, IÑES. I WANT HIM TO FEEL THE HANDS OF THE REAPER ON HIS THROAT IN PUNISHMENT FOR HIS CRIMES.
... ET SPIRITU SANCTI, AMEN.

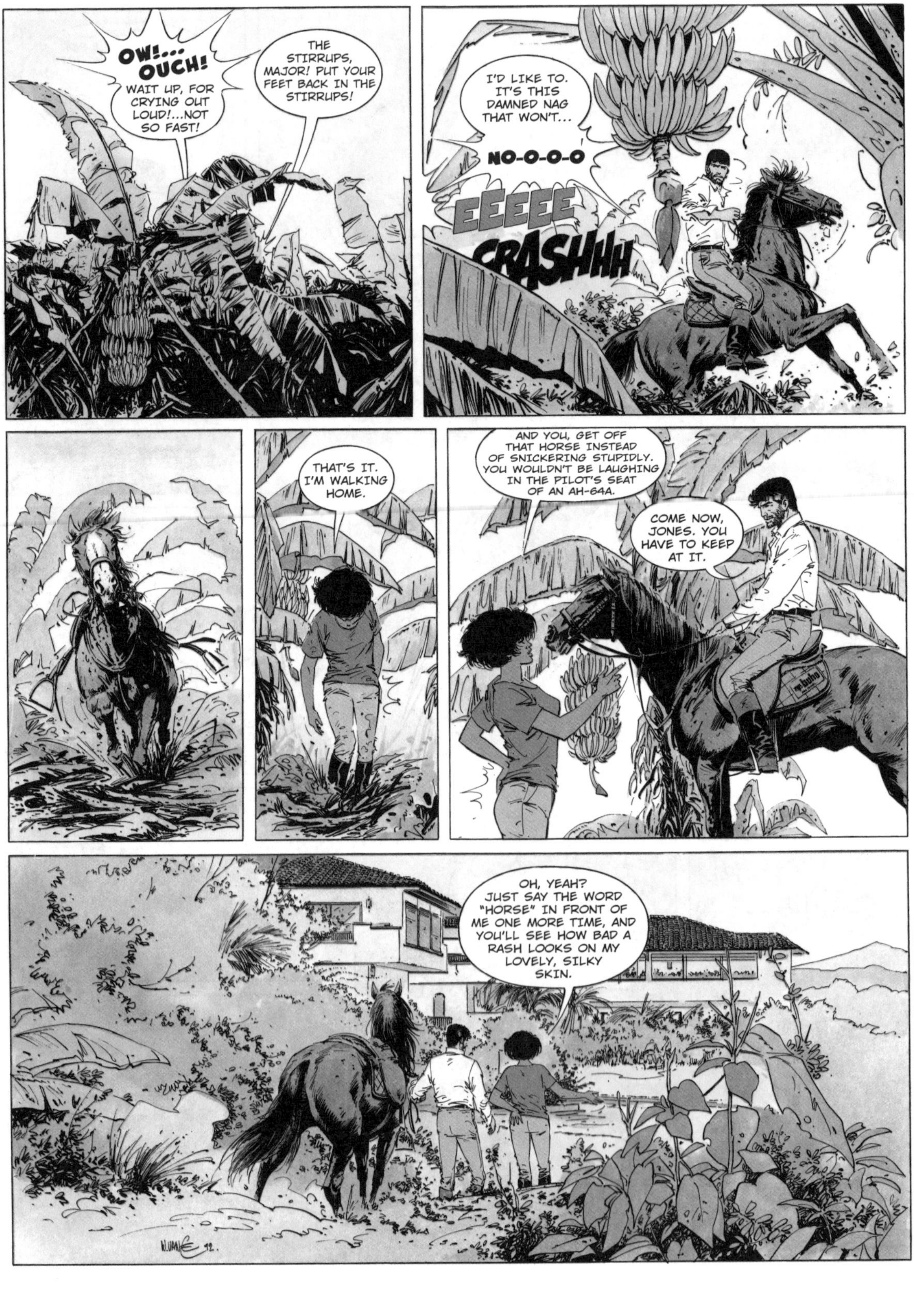
OW!... OUCH! WAIT UP, FOR CRYING OUT LOUD!...NOT SO FAST!
THE STIRRUPS, MAJOR! PUT YOUR FEET BACK IN THE STIRRUPS!
I'D LIKE TO. IT'S THIS DAMNED NAG THAT WON'T...
NO-O-O-O
EEEEE
CRASHHH
THAT'S IT. I'M WALKING HOME.
AND YOU, GET OFF THAT HORSE INSTEAD OF SNICKERING STUPIDLY. YOU WOULDN'T BE LAUGHING IN THE PILOT'S SEAT OF AN AH-64A.
COME NOW, JONES. YOU HAVE TO KEEP AT IT.
OH, YEAH? JUST SAY THE WORD "HORSE" IN FRONT OF ME ONE MORE TIME, AND YOU'LL SEE HOW BAD A RASH LOOKS ON MY LOVELY, SILKY SKIN.

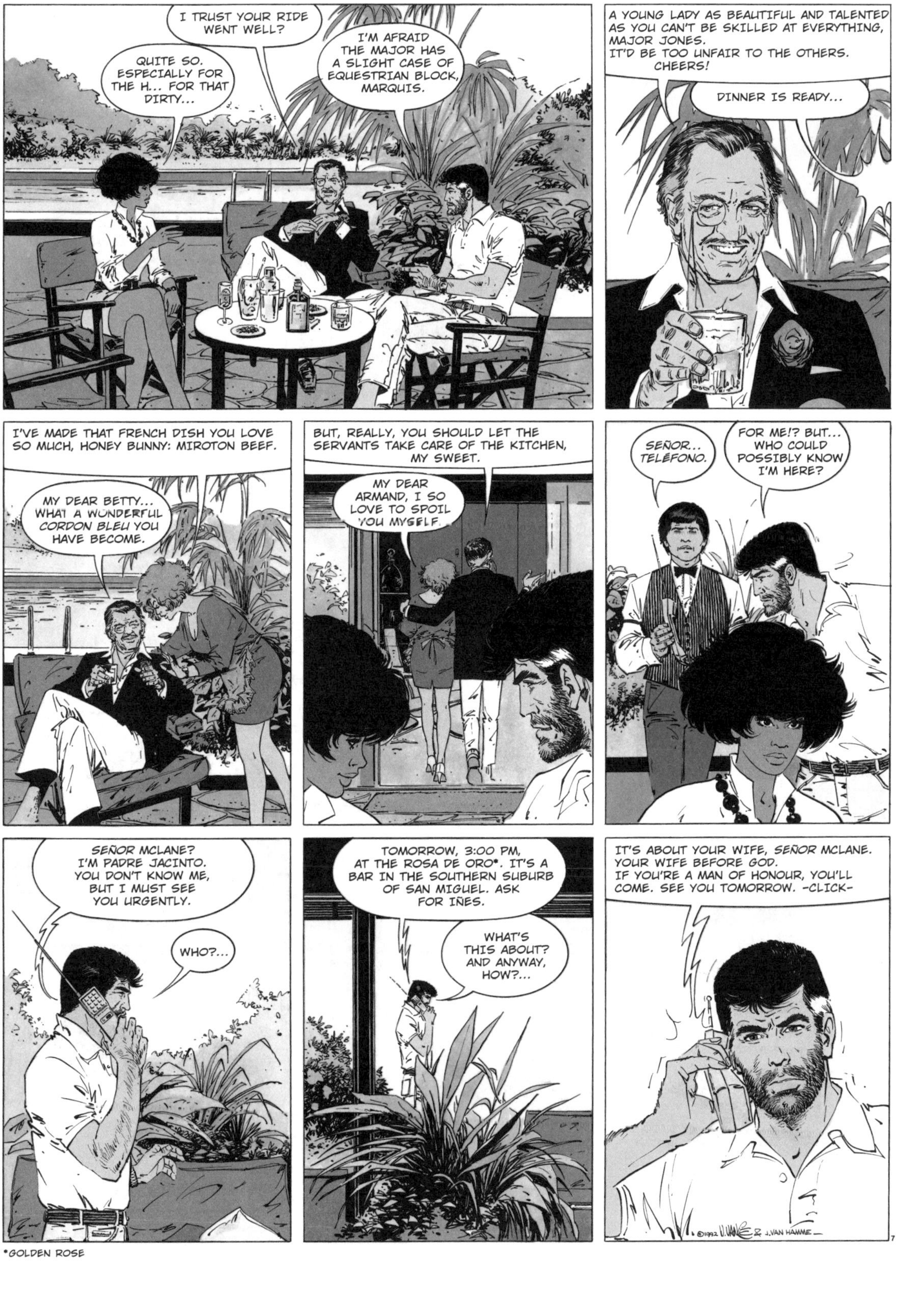
I TRUST YOUR RIDE WENT WELL?
QUITE SO. ESPECIALLY FOR THE H... FOR THAT DIRTY...
I'M AFRAID THE MAJOR HAS A SLIGHT CASE OF EQUESTRIAN BLOCK, MARQUIS.
A YOUNG LADY AS BEAUTIFUL AND TALENTED AS YOU CAN'T BE SKILLED AT EVERYTHING, MAJOR JONES. IT'D BE TOO UNFAIR TO THE OTHERS. CHEERS!
DINNER IS READY...
I'VE MADE THAT FRENCH DISH YOU LOVE SO MUCH, HONEY BUNNY: MIROTON BEEF.
MY DEAR BETTY... WHAT A WONDERFUL CORDON BLEU YOU HAVE BECOME.
BUT, REALLY, YOU SHOULD LET THE SERVANTS TAKE CARE OF THE KITCHEN, MY SWEET.
MY DEAR ARMAND, I SO LOVE TO SPOIL YOU MYSELF.
SEÑOR... TELÉFONO.
FOR ME!? BUT... WHO COULD POSSIBLY KNOW I'M HERE?
SEÑOR MCLANE? I'M PADRE JACINTO. YOU DON'T KNOW ME, BUT I MUST SEE YOU URGENTLY.
WHO?...
TOMORROW, 3:00 PM, AT THE ROSA DE ORO*. IT'S A BAR IN THE SOUTHERN SUBURB OF SAN MIGUEL. ASK FOR IÑES.
WHAT'S THIS ABOUT? AND ANYWAY, HOW?...
IT'S ABOUT YOUR WIFE, SEÑOR MCLANE. YOUR WIFE BEFORE GOD. IF YOU'RE A MAN OF HONOUR, YOU'LL COME. SEE YOU TOMORROW. -CLICK-
©1992 W. VANCE & J. VAN HAMME
7

*GOLDEN ROSE

SO, YOU'RE MARRIED, THEN?
SO IT SEEMS.
TA-DAAAAAAH!... AND NOW, LADIES AND GENTLEMEN, A NEW REVELATION IN THE SECRET AND SENSATIONAL LIFE OF JASON MCLANE, A.K.A. ALAN SMITH, A.K.A. JAKE SHELTON, A.K.A. STEVE ROWLAND, A.K.A. ROSS TANNER, A.K.A....
BITE ME, JONES. YOU'RE NOT FUNNY.
AND YOU'RE TOO GULLIBLE. A STRANGER TELLS YOU SOME COCKAMAMIE STORY ON THE PHONE, AND YOU LOWER YOUR HEAD AND CHARGE STRAIGHT INTO SOMETHING THAT LOOKS LIKE A MAGNITUDE 10 TRAP ON THE JAMES BOND SCALE.
YOU'RE FORGETTING ONE DETAIL...
THERE'S A SIX-YEAR GAP IN MY C.V. A HOLE DURING WHICH I LEARNED SPANISH. EVEN IF THERE'S ONLY A 1 IN 100 CHANCE TO FIND OUT ANYTHING, I WANT TO KNOW.
BESIDES, A LITTLE TRIP TO THE CITY WILL DO US GOOD. I WAS GETTING TIRED OF ONLY SEEING THE BANANA TREES OF PRÉSEAU'S PLANTATION. WHAT HAVE WE GOT TO LOSE, HMM?
WHAT HAVE WE GOT TO LOSE?
NISSAN
NOW YOU'RE THE ONE FORGETTING SOMETHING, XIII: WE STILL HAVE THE MONGOOSE AFTER US, OR WHATEVER OTHER KILLER SHERIDAN MIGHT HAVE SENT.
IF DEAR OLD WALLY HAD WANTED US DEAD, IT WOULD HAVE HAPPENED A LONG TIME AGO. WITH THE MEANS AT HIS DISPOSAL, HE'D HAVE HAD NO TROUBLE LOCATING US AND SENDING A COUPLE OF SNIPERS TO TAKE US OUT.
SAN MIGUEL - EL GALGO
N3
CIUDAD
BUT HE KNOWS NOW THAT WE CAN'T DO ANYTHING AGAINST HIM ANYMORE. IT'D BE STUPID OF HIM TO RISK A NEW INVESTIGATION. AS LONG AS HE'S PRESIDENT AND WE KEEP A LOW PROFILE, WE DON'T HAVE TO WORRY ABOUT HIM.
THAT'S YOUR OPINION.
8

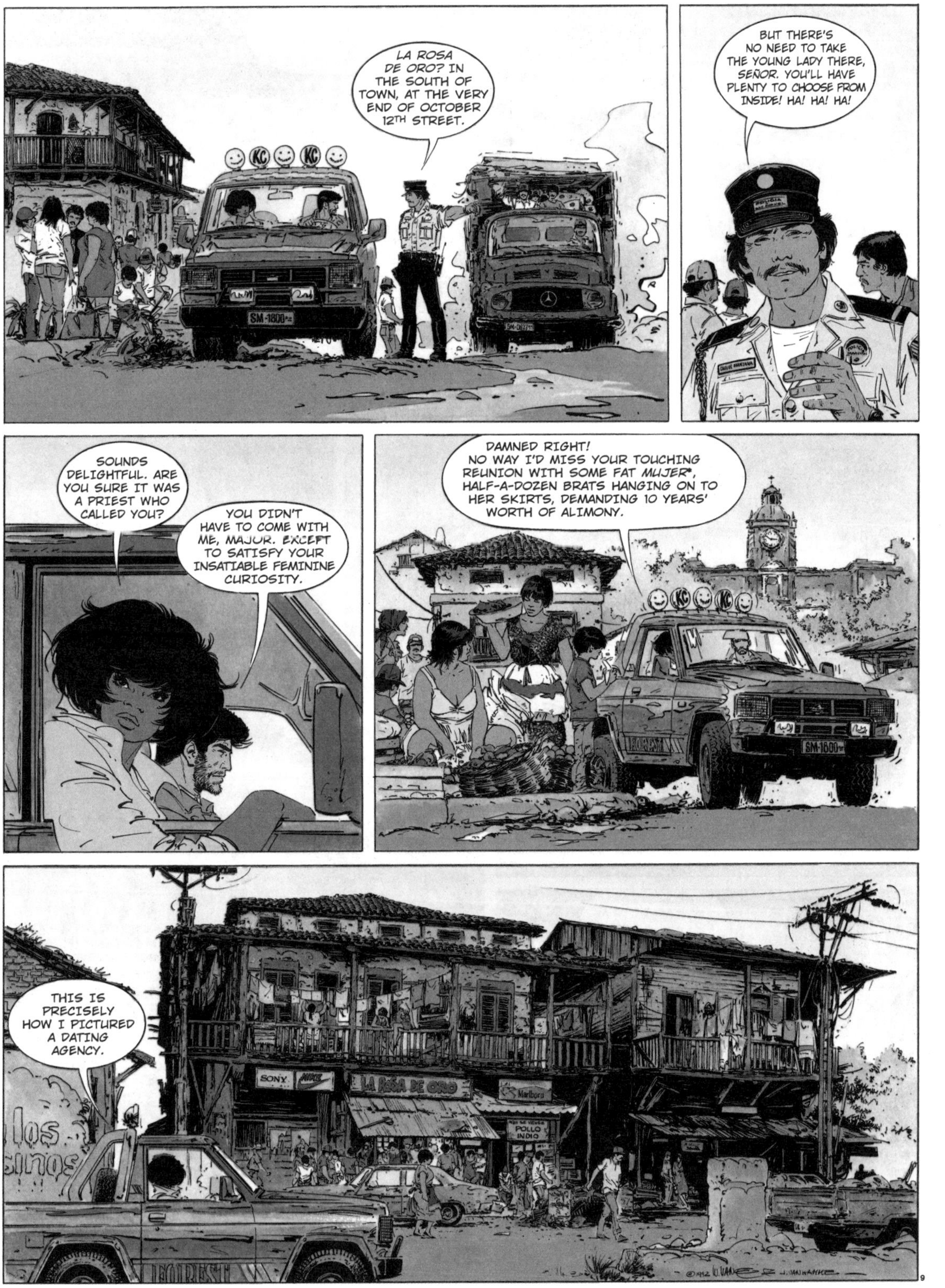
LA ROSA DE ORO? IN THE SOUTH OF TOWN, AT THE VERY END OF OCTOBER 12TH STREET.
BUT THERE'S NO NEED TO TAKE THE YOUNG LADY THERE, SEÑOR. YOU'LL HAVE PLENTY TO CHOOSE FROM INSIDE! HA! HA! HA!
SOUNDS DELIGHTFUL. ARE YOU SURE IT WAS A PRIEST WHO CALLED YOU?
YOU DIDN'T HAVE TO COME WITH ME, MAJOR. EXCEPT TO SATISFY YOUR INSATIABLE FEMININE CURIOSITY.
DAMNED RIGHT! NO WAY I'D MISS YOUR TOUCHING REUNION WITH SOME FAT MUJER*, HALF-A-DOZEN BRATS HANGING ON TO HER SKIRTS, DEMANDING 10 YEARS' WORTH OF ALIMONY.
THIS IS PRECISELY HOW I PICTURED A DATING AGENCY.
SONY
NIKE
LA ROSA DE ORO
Marlboro
POLLO INDIO
9

*WOMAN.

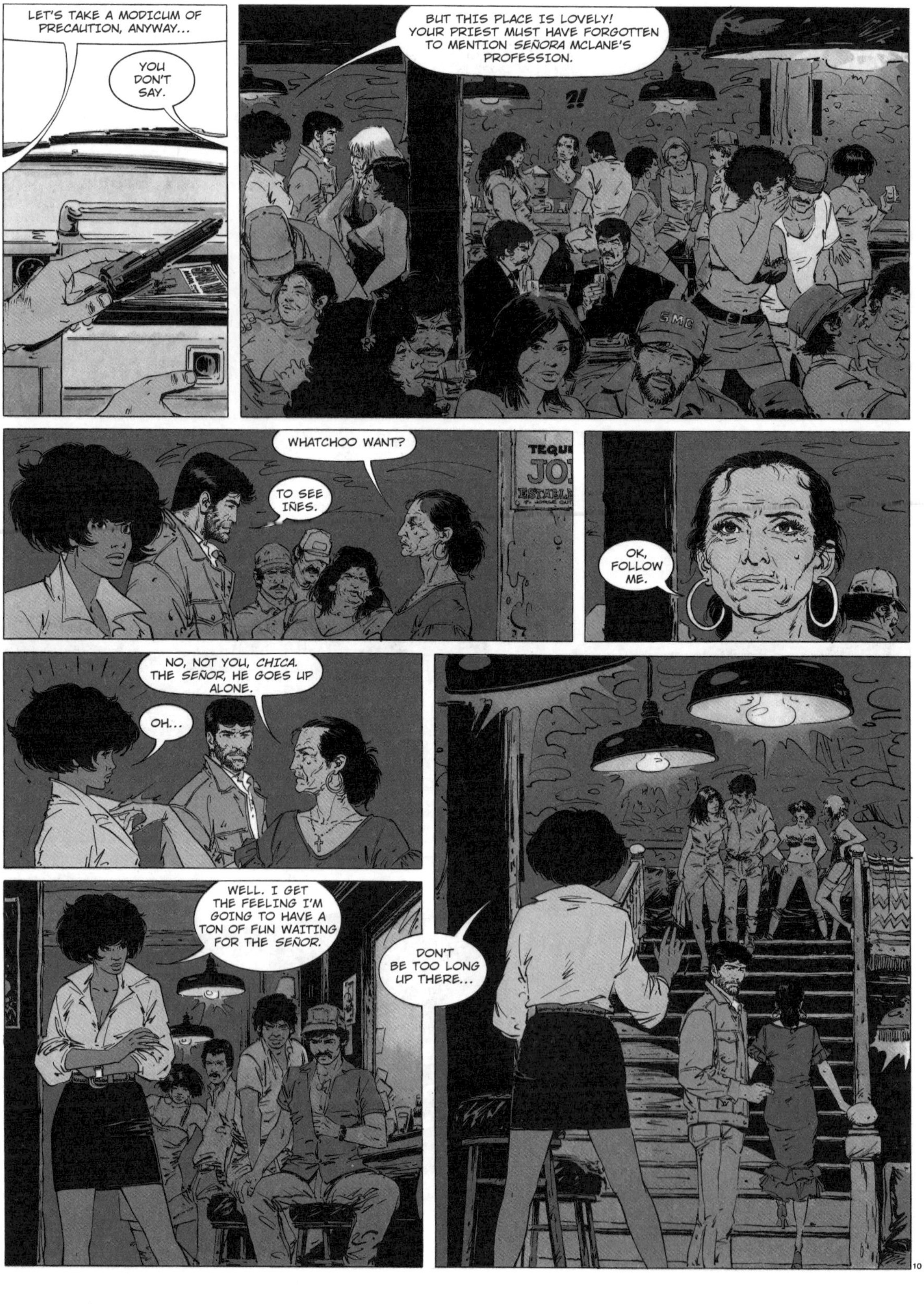
LET'S TAKE A MODICUM OF PRECAUTION, ANYWAY...
YOU DON'T SAY.
BUT THIS PLACE IS LOVELY! YOUR PRIEST MUST HAVE FORGOTTEN TO MENTION SEÑORA MCLANE'S PROFESSION.
?!
WHATCHOO WANT?
TO SEE IÑES.
OK, FOLLOW ME.
NO, NOT YOU, CHICA. THE SEÑOR, HE GOES UP ALONE.
OH...
WELL. I GET THE FEELING I'M GOING TO HAVE A TON OF FUN WAITING FOR THE SEÑOR.
DON'T BE TOO LONG UP THERE...
10

INSIDE, SEÑOR.

BRAVO, SEÑOR MCLANE, YOU'RE ON TIME. LEAVE US, MY CHILD.

HMM... STRANGE. SOMETHING IN THE EYES, MAYBE... AGUARDIENTE? TEQUILA? WHISKY?

NOTHING, THANKS.

THAT'S ONE THING THAT HASN'T CHANGED, AT LEAST: STILL THE SOBER TYPE.

WE'RE SUPPOSED TO KNOW EACH OTHER, THEN?

IF YOU'RE THE ONE I WAS TOLD YOU WERE, THEN WE SPENT A FEW YEARS TOGETHER IN THE COSTA VERDE MOUNTAINS. BUT I WAS ALSO TOLD YOU'D FORGOTTEN. A PITY. SALUD!

TOLD? BY WHOM?

I WAS TOLD, TOO, THAT YOU'D CHANGED YOUR NAME AND YOUR FACE. IT'S TRUE THAT YOU DON'T LOOK LIKE THE MAN I KNEW. BUT MODERN SURGERY CAN PERFORM MIRACLES, CAN'T IT?

YOU DIDN'T ANSWER MY QUESTION, PADRE.

BEFORE I ANSWER IT, I MUST CHECK THAT YOU REALLY ARE THE ONE WHO NOW CALLS HIMSELF JASON MCLANE—AND BEARS A CURIOUS TATTOO ABOVE HIS LEFT CLAVICLE. YOU WON'T MIND SHOWING IT TO ME, WILL YOU?

PERFECT. NOW WE CAN GET DOWN TO BRASS TACKS.

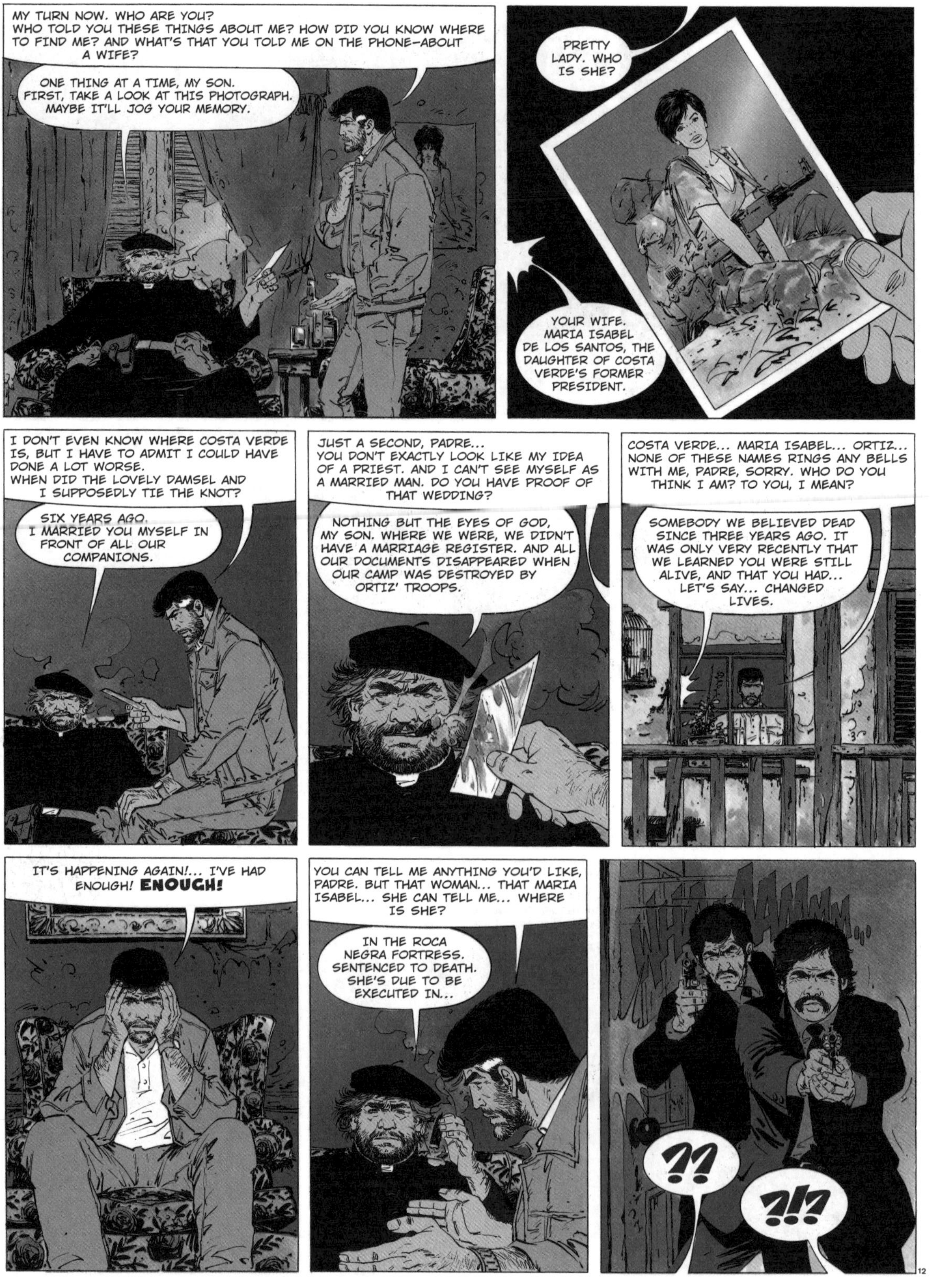
MY TURN NOW. WHO ARE YOU? WHO TOLD YOU THESE THINGS ABOUT ME? HOW DID YOU KNOW WHERE TO FIND ME? AND WHAT'S THAT YOU TOLD ME ON THE PHONE–ABOUT A WIFE?
ONE THING AT A TIME, MY SON. FIRST, TAKE A LOOK AT THIS PHOTOGRAPH. MAYBE IT'LL JOG YOUR MEMORY.
PRETTY LADY. WHO IS SHE?
YOUR WIFE. MARIA ISABEL DE LOS SANTOS, THE DAUGHTER OF COSTA VERDE'S FORMER PRESIDENT.
I DON'T EVEN KNOW WHERE COSTA VERDE IS, BUT I HAVE TO ADMIT I COULD HAVE DONE A LOT WORSE. WHEN DID THE LOVELY DAMSEL AND I SUPPOSEDLY TIE THE KNOT?
SIX YEARS AGO. I MARRIED YOU MYSELF IN FRONT OF ALL OUR COMPANIONS.
JUST A SECOND, PADRE... YOU DON'T EXACTLY LOOK LIKE MY IDEA OF A PRIEST. AND I CAN'T SEE MYSELF AS A MARRIED MAN. DO YOU HAVE PROOF OF THAT WEDDING?
NOTHING BUT THE EYES OF GOD, MY SON. WHERE WE WERE, WE DIDN'T HAVE A MARRIAGE REGISTER. AND ALL OUR DOCUMENTS DISAPPEARED WHEN OUR CAMP WAS DESTROYED BY ORTIZ' TROOPS.
COSTA VERDE... MARIA ISABEL... ORTIZ... NONE OF THESE NAMES RINGS ANY BELLS WITH ME, PADRE, SORRY. WHO DO YOU THINK I AM? TO YOU, I MEAN?
SOMEBODY WE BELIEVED DEAD SINCE THREE YEARS AGO. IT WAS ONLY VERY RECENTLY THAT WE LEARNED YOU WERE STILL ALIVE, AND THAT YOU HAD... LET'S SAY... CHANGED LIVES.
IT'S HAPPENING AGAIN!... I'VE HAD ENOUGH! ENOUGH!
YOU CAN TELL ME ANYTHING YOU'D LIKE, PADRE. BUT THAT WOMAN... THAT MARIA ISABEL... SHE CAN TELL ME... WHERE IS SHE?
IN THE ROCA NEGRA FORTRESS. SENTENCED TO DEATH. SHE'S DUE TO BE EXECUTED IN...
??
?!?

CUENTA...
CUENTA... CUENTA MEEE... PARA LO QUE TE QUIERO ooo...
BANG PAW
BANG BANG
BANG
BANG BANG
DZAINGG
PAW
TCHAK
DON'T LET HIM GET AWAY!
BANG BANG
PAW PAW

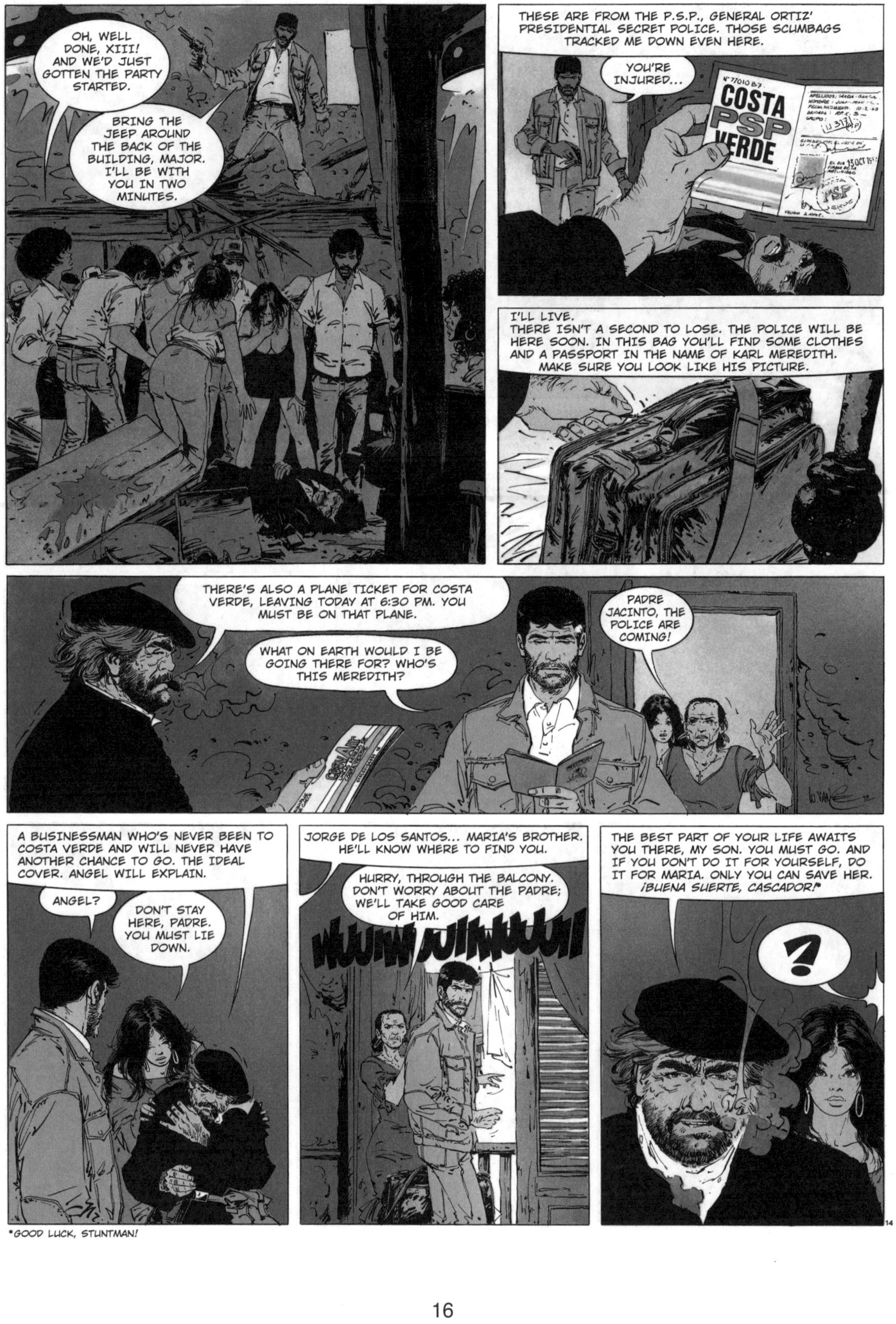
OH, WELL DONE, XIII! AND WE'D JUST GOTTEN THE PARTY STARTED.
BRING THE JEEP AROUND THE BACK OF THE BUILDING, MAJOR. I'LL BE WITH YOU IN TWO MINUTES.
THESE ARE FROM THE P.S.P., GENERAL ORTIZ' PRESIDENTIAL SECRET POLICE. THOSE SCUMBAGS TRACKED ME DOWN EVEN HERE.
YOU'RE INJURED...
COSTA PSP VERDE
I'LL LIVE.
THERE ISN'T A SECOND TO LOSE. THE POLICE WILL BE HERE SOON. IN THIS BAG YOU'LL FIND SOME CLOTHES AND A PASSPORT IN THE NAME OF KARL MEREDITH. MAKE SURE YOU LOOK LIKE HIS PICTURE.
THERE'S ALSO A PLANE TICKET FOR COSTA VERDE, LEAVING TODAY AT 6:30 PM. YOU MUST BE ON THAT PLANE.
WHAT ON EARTH WOULD I BE GOING THERE FOR? WHO'S THIS MEREDITH?
PADRE JACINTO, THE POLICE ARE COMING!
A BUSINESSMAN WHO'S NEVER BEEN TO COSTA VERDE AND WILL NEVER HAVE ANOTHER CHANCE TO GO. THE IDEAL COVER. ANGEL WILL EXPLAIN.
ANGEL?
DON'T STAY HERE, PADRE. YOU MUST LIE DOWN.
JORGE DE LOS SANTOS... MARIA'S BROTHER. HE'LL KNOW WHERE TO FIND YOU.
HURRY, THROUGH THE BALCONY. DON'T WORRY ABOUT THE PADRE; WE'LL TAKE GOOD CARE OF HIM.
THE BEST PART OF YOUR LIFE AWAITS YOU THERE, MY SON. YOU MUST GO. AND IF YOU DON'T DO IT FOR YOURSELF, DO IT FOR MARIA. ONLY YOU CAN SAVE HER. ¡BUENA SUERTE, CASCADOR!*
?

*GOOD LUCK, STUNTMAN!

WUIIWUIIWUUIIII
RAMON! PABLO! GO AROUND THE BACK AND CUFF ANYTHING THAT MOVES! THE REST OF YOU, WITH ME!
SONY
NIKE
LA ROSA DE ORO
Marlboro
POLLO
POLICIA
HEY, YOU! WHAT ARE YOU DOING HERE?
KC
I'M NOT DOING ANYTHING WRONG, OFFICER.
YOU'RE NOT FROM AROUND HERE, YOU. COME ON—OUT, SO I CAN GET A CLOSER LOOK.
HMPFFF
ME JANE, YOU TARZAN, IS THAT IT? HOW ABOUT EXPLAINING THE RULES OF THIS GAME?
LATER, JONES. FIRST, LET'S GET THE HELL OUT OF HERE.
SM-1800
??
EEEEE
©1992 VANCE & J. VAN HAMME
15

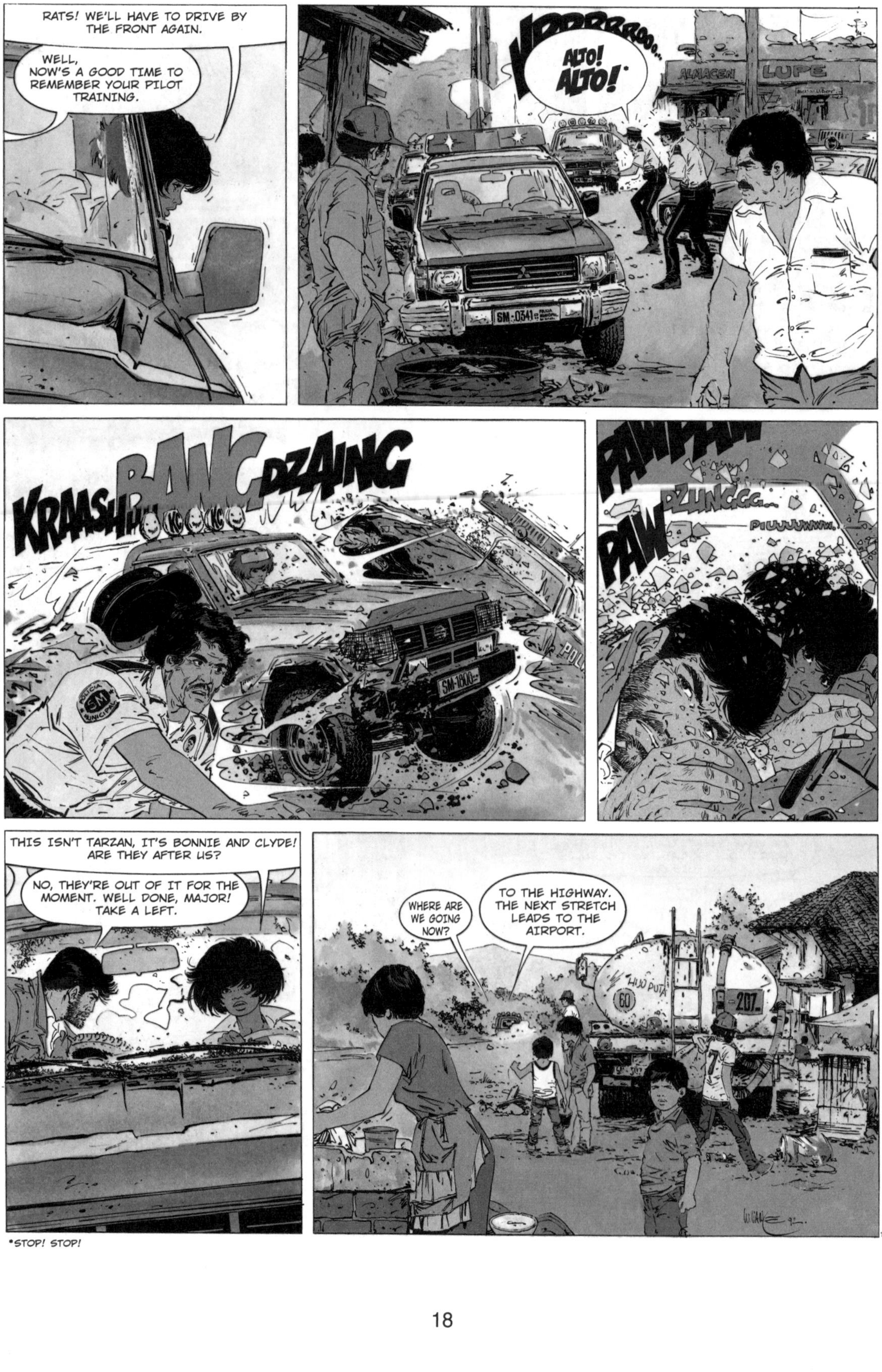
RATS! WE'LL HAVE TO DRIVE BY THE FRONT AGAIN.
WELL, NOW'S A GOOD TIME TO REMEMBER YOUR PILOT TRAINING.
VRRRRRROOO...
ALTO! ALTO!*
ALMACEN
LUPE
SM-0341
KRAASH BANG DZAING
SM-1800
PAW PAW
PAW
DZUNGGG...
PIUUUUWWW...
THIS ISN'T TARZAN, IT'S BONNIE AND CLYDE! ARE THEY AFTER US?
NO, THEY'RE OUT OF IT FOR THE MOMENT. WELL DONE, MAJOR! TAKE A LEFT.
WHERE ARE WE GOING NOW?
TO THE HIGHWAY. THE NEXT STRETCH LEADS TO THE AIRPORT.
207
60
16

*STOP! STOP!

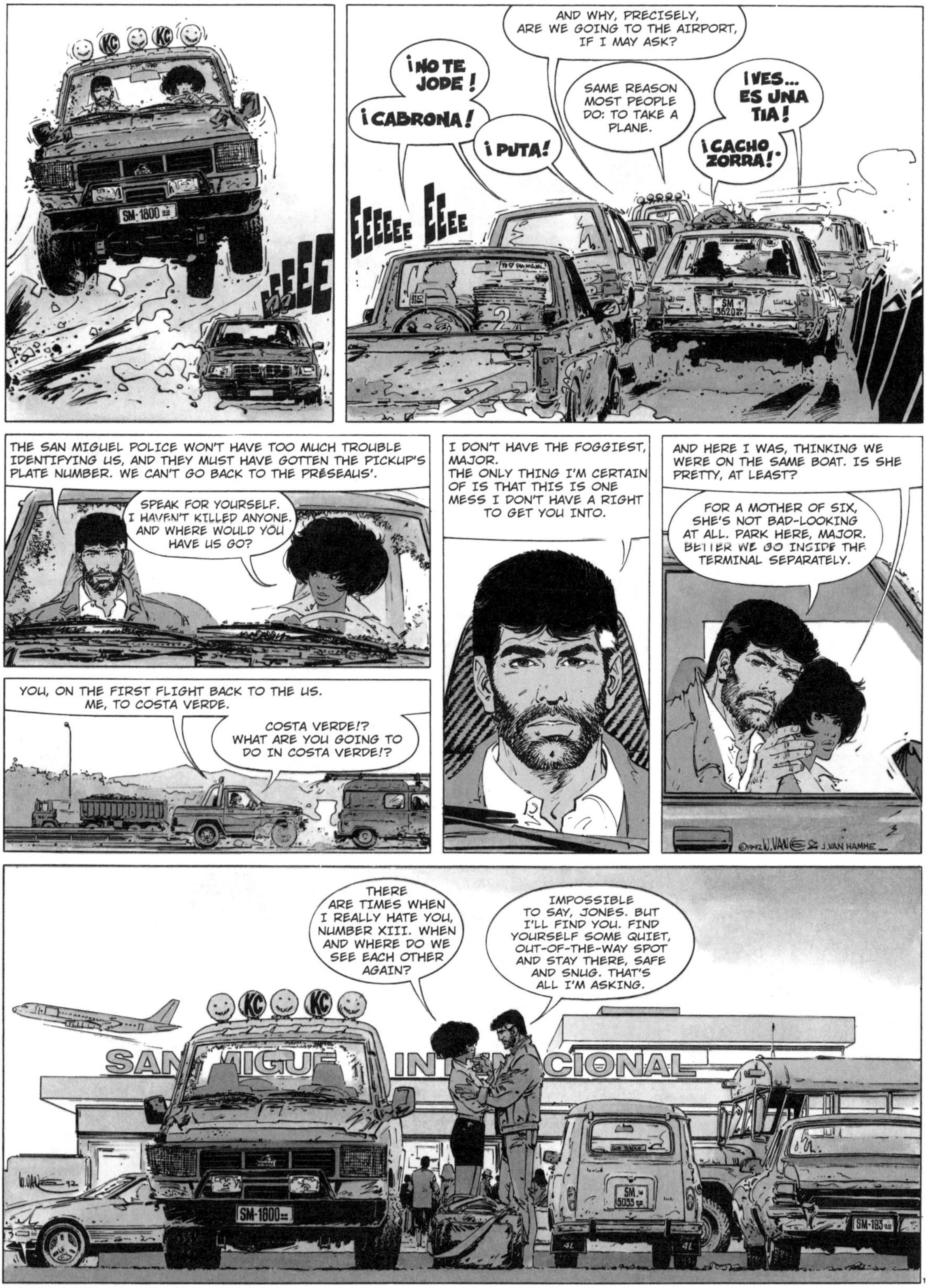
EEEE
EEEEEE EEee
AND WHY, PRECISELY, ARE WE GOING TO THE AIRPORT, IF I MAY ASK?
¡NO TE JODE!
¡CABRONA!
¡PUTA!
SAME REASON MOST PEOPLE DO: TO TAKE A PLANE.
¡VES... ES UNA TIA!
¡CACHO ZORRA!*
THE SAN MIGUEL POLICE WON'T HAVE TOO MUCH TROUBLE IDENTIFYING US, AND THEY MUST HAVE GOTTEN THE PICKUP'S PLATE NUMBER. WE CAN'T GO BACK TO THE PRÉSEAUS'.
SPEAK FOR YOURSELF. I HAVEN'T KILLED ANYONE. AND WHERE WOULD YOU HAVE US GO?
YOU, ON THE FIRST FLIGHT BACK TO THE US. ME, TO COSTA VERDE.
COSTA VERDE!? WHAT ARE YOU GOING TO DO IN COSTA VERDE!?
I DON'T HAVE THE FOGGIEST, MAJOR. THE ONLY THING I'M CERTAIN OF IS THAT THIS IS ONE MESS I DON'T HAVE A RIGHT TO GET YOU INTO.
AND HERE I WAS, THINKING WE WERE ON THE SAME BOAT. IS SHE PRETTY, AT LEAST?
FOR A MOTHER OF SIX, SHE'S NOT BAD-LOOKING AT ALL. PARK HERE, MAJOR. BETTER WE GO INSIDE THE TERMINAL SEPARATELY.
©1992 W. VANCE & J. VAN HAMME
THERE ARE TIMES WHEN I REALLY HATE YOU, NUMBER XIII. WHEN AND WHERE DO WE SEE EACH OTHER AGAIN?
IMPOSSIBLE TO SAY, JONES. BUT I'LL FIND YOU. FIND YOURSELF SOME QUIET, OUT-OF-THE-WAY SPOT AND STAY THERE, SAFE AND SNUG. THAT'S ALL I'M ASKING.
SAN MIGUEL INTERNACIONAL
SM-1800
17

* VARIOUS RUDE AND UNPRINTABLE EPITHETS...

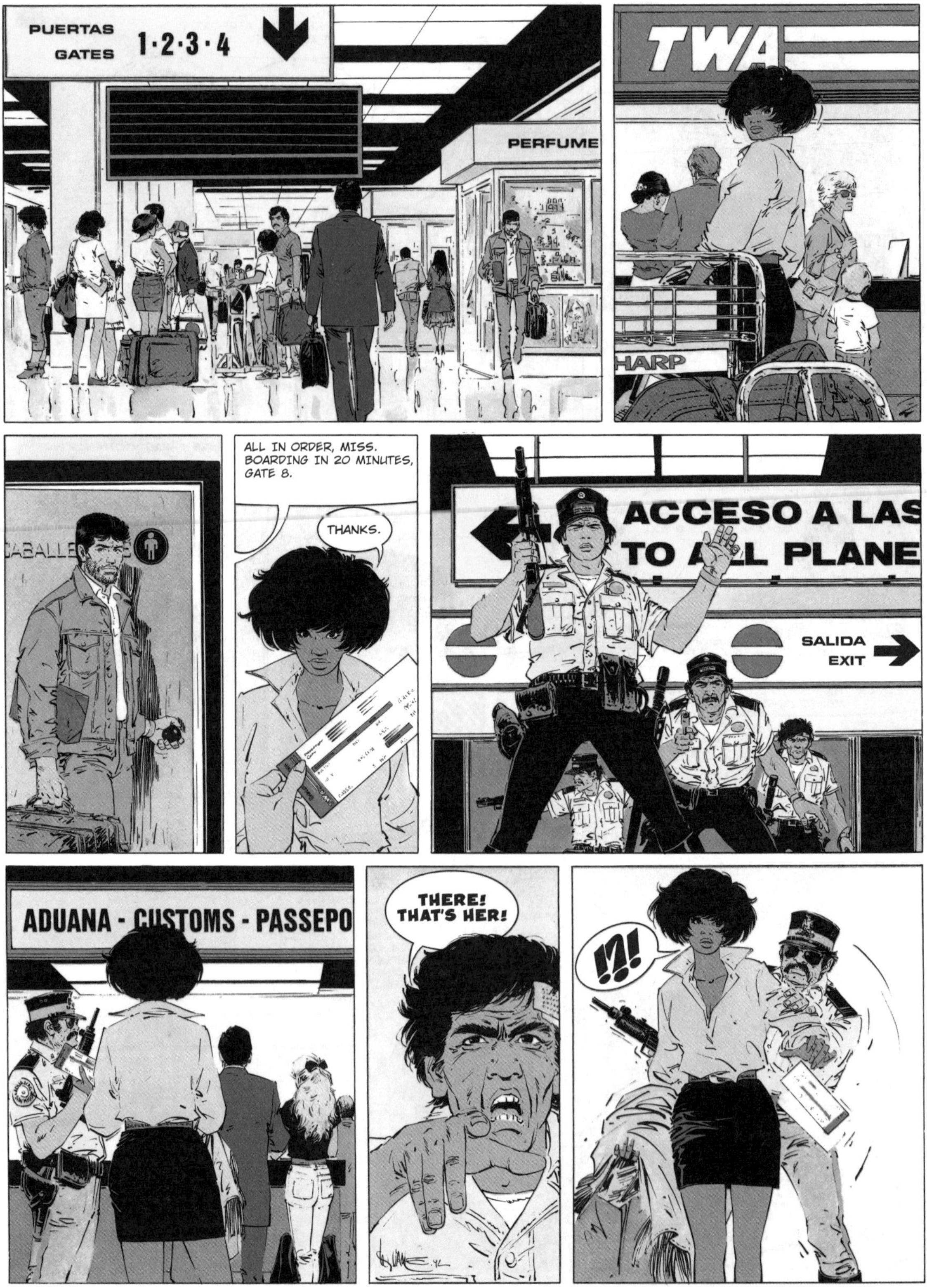

PUERTAS
GATES
1·2·3·4
PERFUME
TWA
HARP
CABALLE
ALL IN ORDER, MISS. BOARDING IN 20 MINUTES, GATE 8.
THANKS.
ACCESO A LAS
TO ALL PLANE
SALIDA
EXIT
ADUANA - CUSTOMS - PASSEPO
THERE! THAT'S HER!
!?!
18

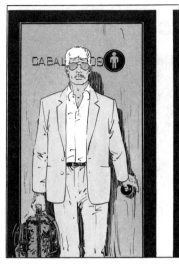

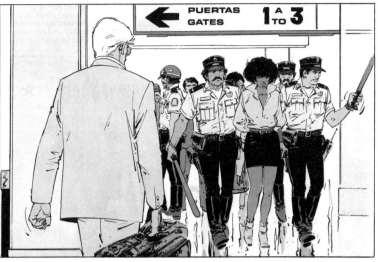

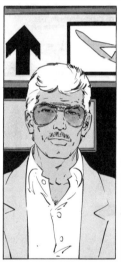

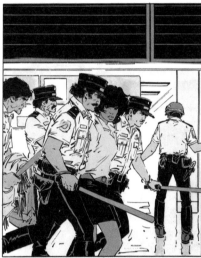

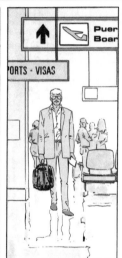

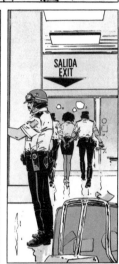

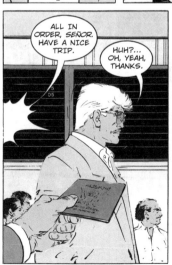

PUERTAS
GATES
1 A TO 3
SALIDA
EXIT
ALL IN ORDER, SEÑOR. HAVE A NICE TRIP.
HUH?... OH, YEAH, THANKS.
IS THIS YOUR FIRST TRIP TO COSTA VERDE?
ER... YES.
J. VAN HAMME

19

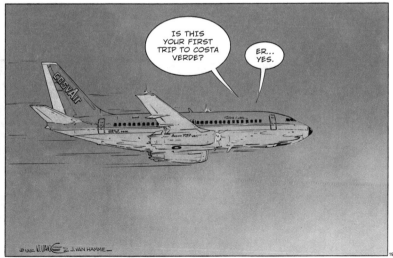

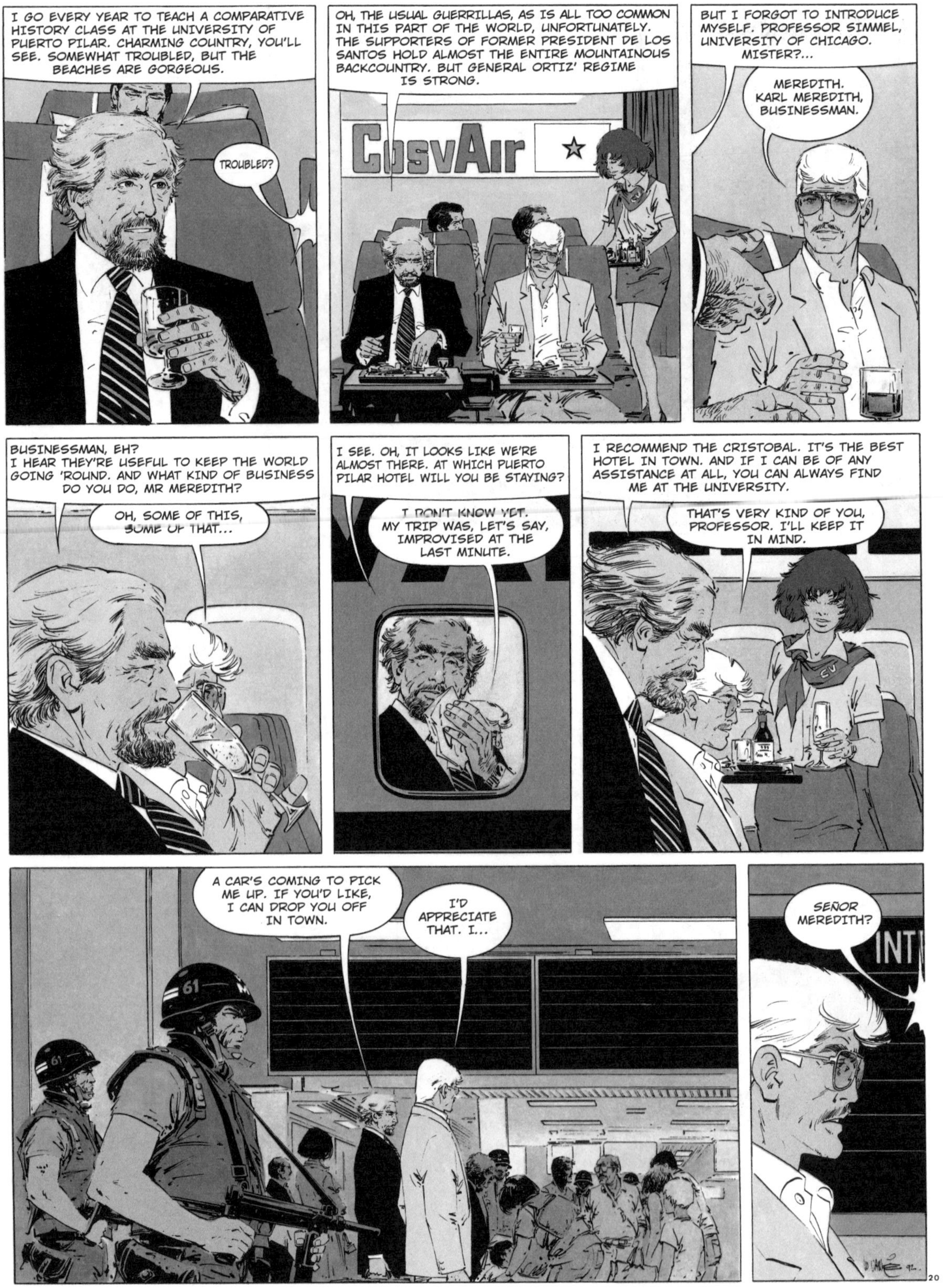

I GO EVERY YEAR TO TEACH A COMPARATIVE HISTORY CLASS AT THE UNIVERSITY OF PUERTO PILAR. CHARMING COUNTRY, YOU'LL SEE. SOMEWHAT TROUBLED, BUT THE BEACHES ARE GORGEOUS.
TROUBLED?
OH, THE USUAL GUERRILLAS, AS IS ALL TOO COMMON IN THIS PART OF THE WORLD, UNFORTUNATELY. THE SUPPORTERS OF FORMER PRESIDENT DE LOS SANTOS HOLD ALMOST THE ENTIRE MOUNTAINOUS BACKCOUNTRY. BUT GENERAL ORTIZ' REGIME IS STRONG.
CosvAir
BUT I FORGOT TO INTRODUCE MYSELF. PROFESSOR SIMMEL, UNIVERSITY OF CHICAGO. MISTER?...
MEREDITH. KARL MEREDITH, BUSINESSMAN.
BUSINESSMAN, EH? I HEAR THEY'RE USEFUL TO KEEP THE WORLD GOING 'ROUND. AND WHAT KIND OF BUSINESS DO YOU DO, MR MEREDITH?
OH, SOME OF THIS, SOME OF THAT...
I SEE. OH, IT LOOKS LIKE WE'RE ALMOST THERE. AT WHICH PUERTO PILAR HOTEL WILL YOU BE STAYING?
I DON'T KNOW YET. MY TRIP WAS, LET'S SAY, IMPROVISED AT THE LAST MINUTE.
I RECOMMEND THE CRISTOBAL. IT'S THE BEST HOTEL IN TOWN. AND IF I CAN BE OF ANY ASSISTANCE AT ALL, YOU CAN ALWAYS FIND ME AT THE UNIVERSITY.
THAT'S VERY KIND OF YOU, PROFESSOR. I'LL KEEP IT IN MIND.
A CAR'S COMING TO PICK ME UP. IF YOU'D LIKE, I CAN DROP YOU OFF IN TOWN.
I'D APPRECIATE THAT. I...
SEÑOR MEREDITH?
20

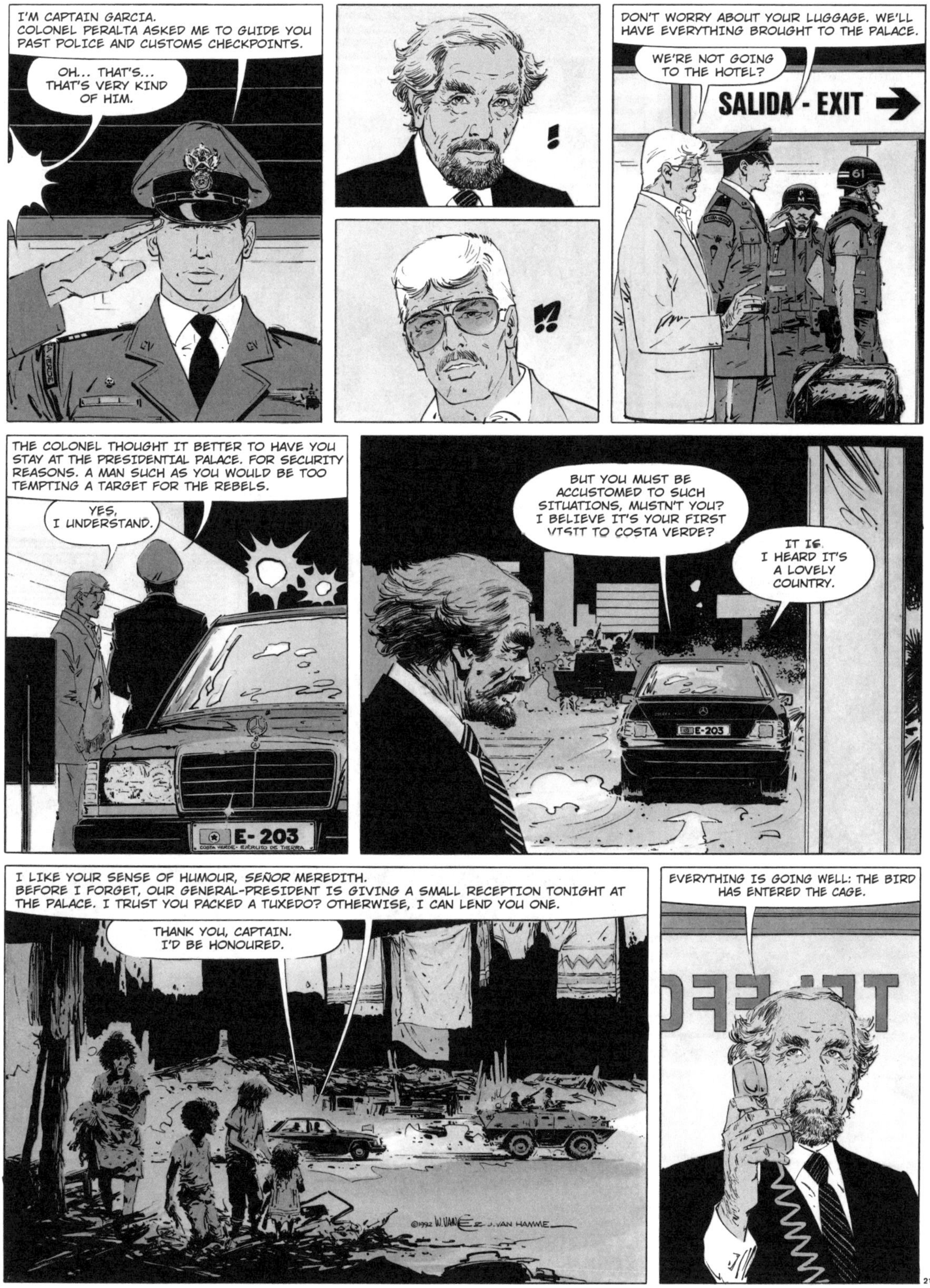

I'M CAPTAIN GARCIA. COLONEL PERALTA ASKED ME TO GUIDE YOU PAST POLICE AND CUSTOMS CHECKPOINTS.
OH... THAT'S... THAT'S VERY KIND OF HIM.
!
!?
DON'T WORRY ABOUT YOUR LUGGAGE. WE'LL HAVE EVERYTHING BROUGHT TO THE PALACE.
WE'RE NOT GOING TO THE HOTEL?
SALIDA - EXIT
THE COLONEL THOUGHT IT BETTER TO HAVE YOU STAY AT THE PRESIDENTIAL PALACE. FOR SECURITY REASONS. A MAN SUCH AS YOU WOULD BE TOO TEMPTING A TARGET FOR THE REBELS.
YES, I UNDERSTAND.
E-203
BUT YOU MUST BE ACCUSTOMED TO SUCH SITUATIONS, MUSTN'T YOU? I BELIEVE IT'S YOUR FIRST VISIT TO COSTA VERDE?
IT IS. I HEARD IT'S A LOVELY COUNTRY.
I LIKE YOUR SENSE OF HUMOUR, SEÑOR MEREDITH. BEFORE I FORGET, OUR GENERAL-PRESIDENT IS GIVING A SMALL RECEPTION TONIGHT AT THE PALACE. I TRUST YOU PACKED A TUXEDO? OTHERWISE, I CAN LEND YOU ONE.
THANK YOU, CAPTAIN. I'D BE HONOURED.
©1992 W. VANCE & J. VAN HAMME
EVERYTHING IS GOING WELL: THE BIRD HAS ENTERED THE CAGE.

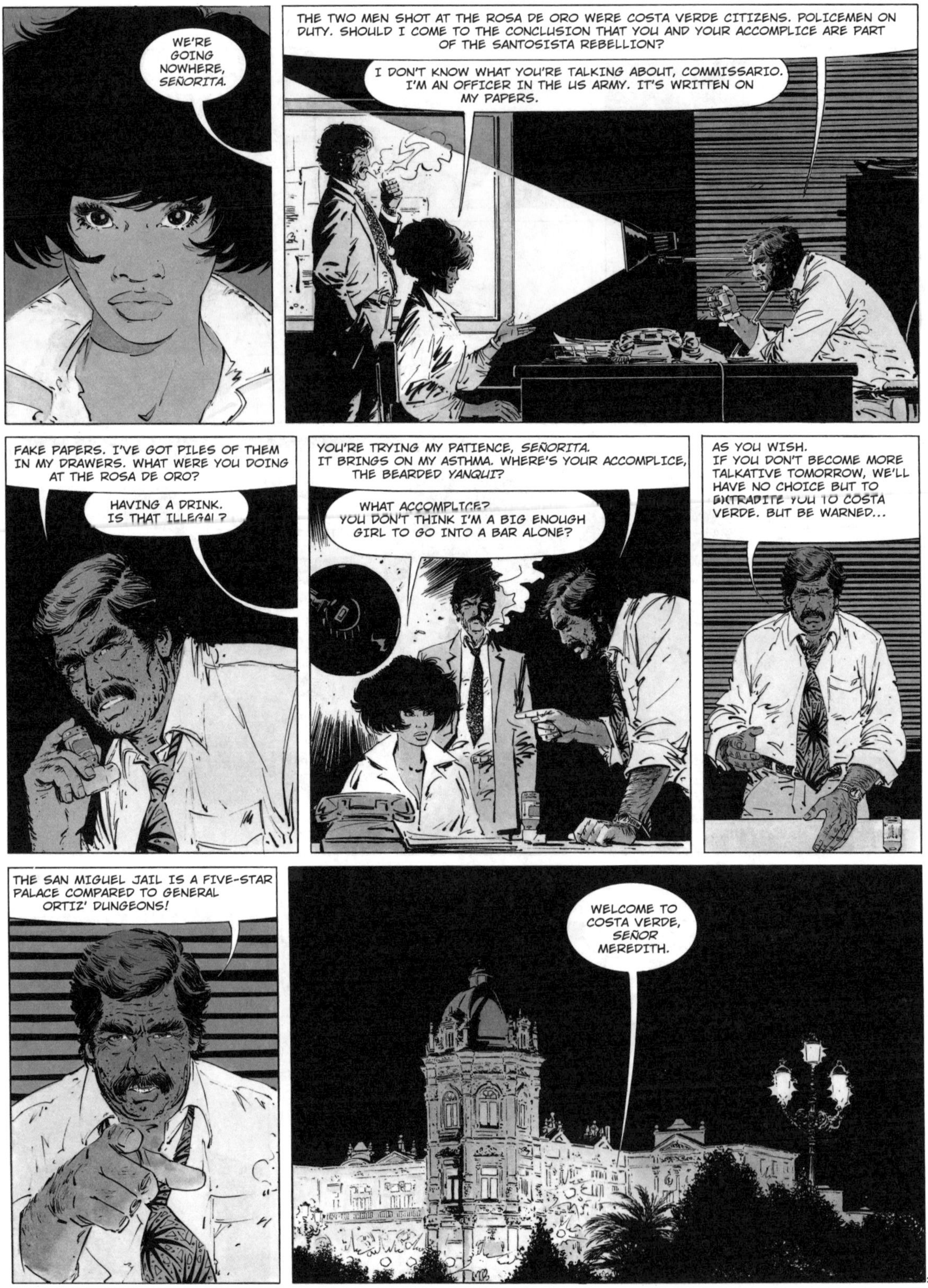

WE'RE GOING NOWHERE, SEÑORITA.
THE TWO MEN SHOT AT THE ROSA DE ORO WERE COSTA VERDE CITIZENS. POLICEMEN ON DUTY. SHOULD I COME TO THE CONCLUSION THAT YOU AND YOUR ACCOMPLICE ARE PART OF THE SANTOSISTA REBELLION?
I DON'T KNOW WHAT YOU'RE TALKING ABOUT, COMMISSARIO. I'M AN OFFICER IN THE US ARMY. IT'S WRITTEN ON MY PAPERS.
FAKE PAPERS. I'VE GOT PILES OF THEM IN MY DRAWERS. WHAT WERE YOU DOING AT THE ROSA DE ORO?
HAVING A DRINK. IS THAT ILLEGAL?
YOU'RE TRYING MY PATIENCE, SEÑORITA. IT BRINGS ON MY ASTHMA. WHERE'S YOUR ACCOMPLICE, THE BEARDED YANQUI?
WHAT ACCOMPLICE? YOU DON'T THINK I'M A BIG ENOUGH GIRL TO GO INTO A BAR ALONE?
AS YOU WISH. IF YOU DON'T BECOME MORE TALKATIVE TOMORROW, WE'LL HAVE NO CHOICE BUT TO EXTRADITE YOU TO COSTA VERDE. BUT BE WARNED...
THE SAN MIGUEL JAIL IS A FIVE-STAR PALACE COMPARED TO GENERAL ORTIZ' DUNGEONS!
WELCOME TO COSTA VERDE, SEÑOR MEREDITH.
22

I'M CERTAIN YOU AND COLONEL PERALTA WILL DO GREAT WORK TOGETHER.

I'M SURE WE WILL TOO, EXCELLENCY.

GENERAL ORTIZ IS AN EXCEPTIONAL STATESMAN WHO WORKS TIRELESSLY FOR HIS COUNTRY. ALL OF US HERE REVERE HIM AS OUR UNQUESTIONED LEADER.

I DON'T DOUBT IT, COLONEL.

AND THANKS TO YOU, SEÑOR MEREDITH, WE WILL FINALLY BE ABLE TO GIVE THE COUP DE GRACE TO THAT DAMNED REBELLION. IT'S BEEN SLOWING OUR PROGRESS FOR SO MANY YEARS NOW.

THANKS TO M...? YES, OF COURSE.

I HAD NO IDEA YOU SPOKE SPANISH SO WELL. THIS WILL MAKE OUR TALKS MUCH EASIER. BUT WE'LL WORRY ABOUT ALL THAT TOMORROW. I'LL LET YOU HAVE FUN TONIGHT TO OUR SUCCESS, SEÑOR.

TO OUR SUCCESS, COLONEL.

BY THE WAY, HAS YOUR LUGGAGE ARRIVED?

NO, NOT YET.

BAH, IT SHOULDN'T BE MUCH LONGER. IN THE MEANTIME, IF YOU NEED ANYTHING, CAPTAIN GARCIA IS AT YOUR ENTIRE DISPOSAL.

HAVE A GOOD EVENING, SEÑOR MEREDITH.

WELL, WHAT A NICE SURPRISE...

I DIDN'T EXPECT TO SEE YOU AGAIN SO SOON. DO YOU ENJOY SOCIETY EVENTS, MR MEREDITH?

ONLY AS PART OF MY PROFESSIONAL DUTIES. WHAT ABOUT YOU, PROFESSOR?

I'M HERE AS AN OBSERVER. I FIND THE SPLENDOUR OF THIS ISLET OF WEALTH, LOST IN AN OCEAN OF POVERTY, FASCINATING. THE AIM OF THE GAME IS TO PREDICT WHEN THIS IMBALANCE WILL REACH THE CRITICAL POINT THAT PRECEDES AN EXPLOSION.

23

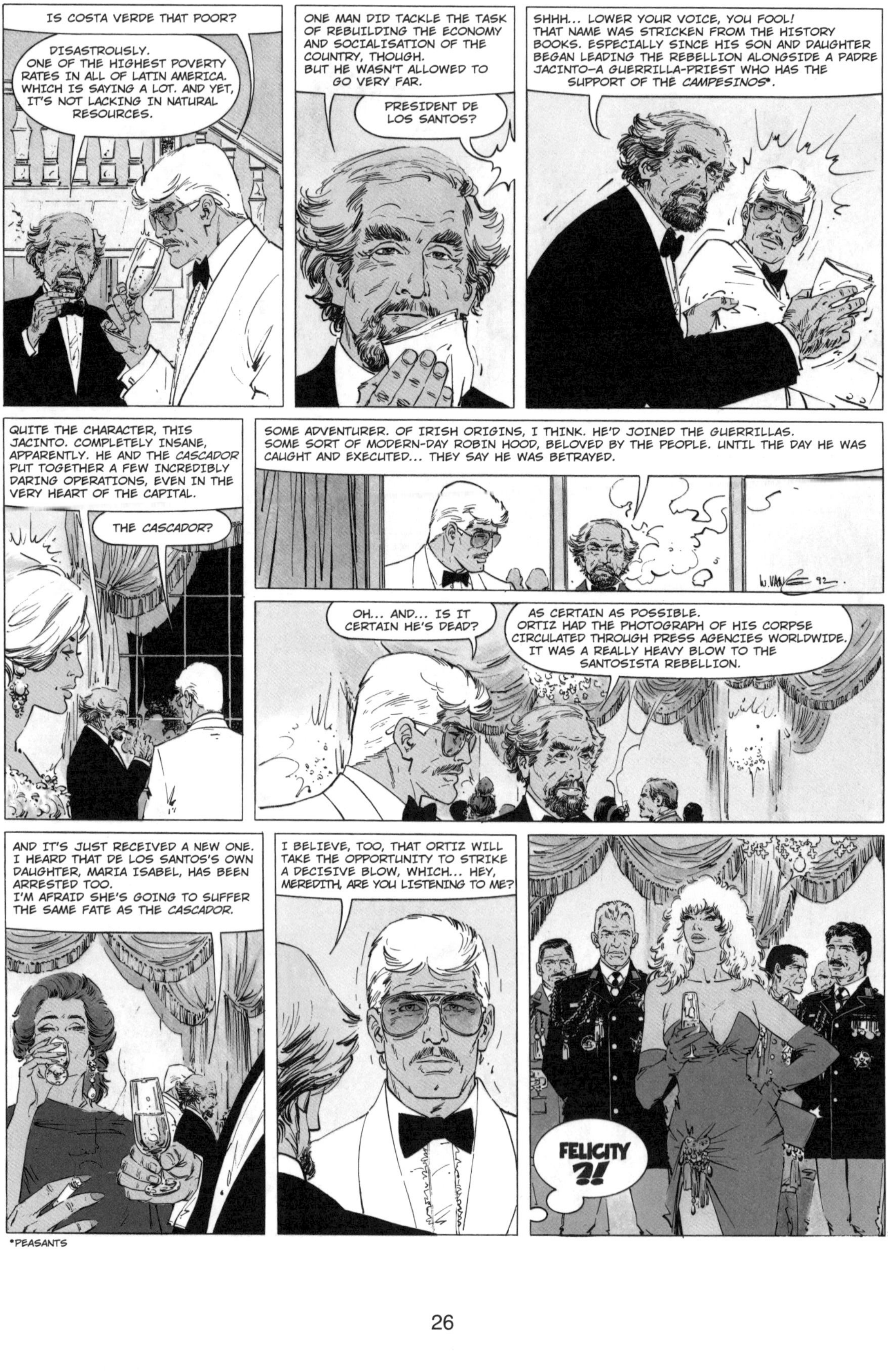
IS COSTA VERDE THAT POOR?
DISASTROUSLY. ONE OF THE HIGHEST POVERTY RATES IN ALL OF LATIN AMERICA. WHICH IS SAYING A LOT. AND YET, IT'S NOT LACKING IN NATURAL RESOURCES.
ONE MAN DID TACKLE THE TASK OF REBUILDING THE ECONOMY AND SOCIALISATION OF THE COUNTRY, THOUGH. BUT HE WASN'T ALLOWED TO GO VERY FAR.
PRESIDENT DE LOS SANTOS?
SHHH... LOWER YOUR VOICE, YOU FOOL! THAT NAME WAS STRICKEN FROM THE HISTORY BOOKS. ESPECIALLY SINCE HIS SON AND DAUGHTER BEGAN LEADING THE REBELLION ALONGSIDE A PADRE JACINTO–A GUERRILLA-PRIEST WHO HAS THE SUPPORT OF THE CAMPESINOS*.
QUITE THE CHARACTER, THIS JACINTO. COMPLETELY INSANE, APPARENTLY. HE AND THE CASCADOR PUT TOGETHER A FEW INCREDIBLY DARING OPERATIONS, EVEN IN THE VERY HEART OF THE CAPITAL.
THE CASCADOR?
SOME ADVENTURER. OF IRISH ORIGINS, I THINK. HE'D JOINED THE GUERRILLAS. SOME SORT OF MODERN-DAY ROBIN HOOD, BELOVED BY THE PEOPLE. UNTIL THE DAY HE WAS CAUGHT AND EXECUTED... THEY SAY HE WAS BETRAYED.
W. VANCE 92.
OH... AND... IS IT CERTAIN HE'S DEAD?
AS CERTAIN AS POSSIBLE. ORTIZ HAD THE PHOTOGRAPH OF HIS CORPSE CIRCULATED THROUGH PRESS AGENCIES WORLDWIDE. IT WAS A REALLY HEAVY BLOW TO THE SANTOSISTA REBELLION.
AND IT'S JUST RECEIVED A NEW ONE. I HEARD THAT DE LOS SANTOS'S OWN DAUGHTER, MARIA ISABEL, HAS BEEN ARRESTED TOO. I'M AFRAID SHE'S GOING TO SUFFER THE SAME FATE AS THE CASCADOR.
I BELIEVE, TOO, THAT ORTIZ WILL TAKE THE OPPORTUNITY TO STRIKE A DECISIVE BLOW, WHICH... HEY, MEREDITH, ARE YOU LISTENING TO ME?
FELICITY ?!
24

*PEASANTS

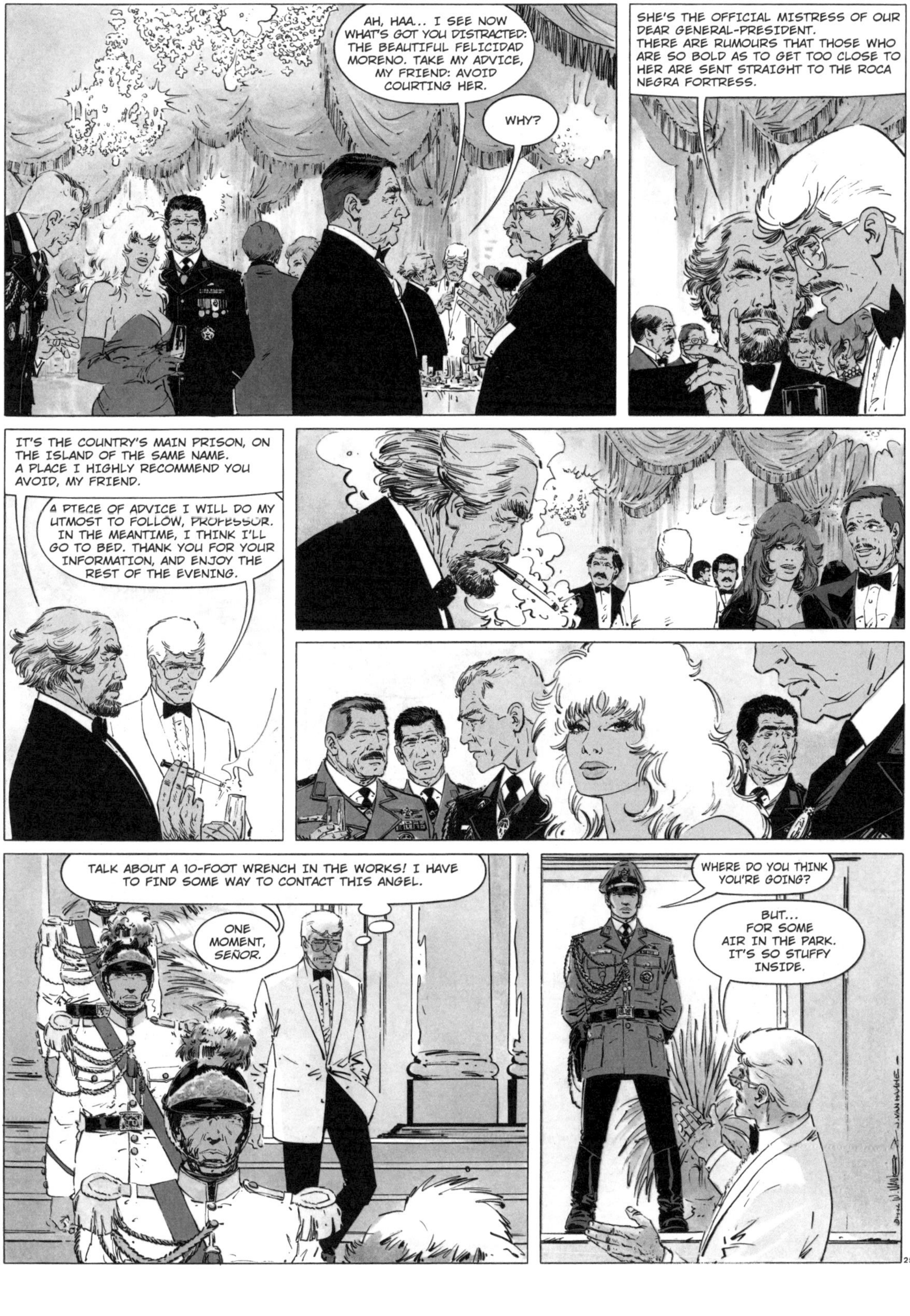
AH, HAA... I SEE NOW WHAT'S GOT YOU DISTRACTED: THE BEAUTIFUL FELICIDAD MORENO. TAKE MY ADVICE, MY FRIEND: AVOID COURTING HER.
WHY?
SHE'S THE OFFICIAL MISTRESS OF OUR DEAR GENERAL-PRESIDENT.
THERE ARE RUMOURS THAT THOSE WHO ARE SO BOLD AS TO GET TOO CLOSE TO HER ARE SENT STRAIGHT TO THE ROCA NEGRA FORTRESS.
IT'S THE COUNTRY'S MAIN PRISON, ON THE ISLAND OF THE SAME NAME.
A PLACE I HIGHLY RECOMMEND YOU AVOID, MY FRIEND.
A PIECE OF ADVICE I WILL DO MY UTMOST TO FOLLOW, PROFESSOR. IN THE MEANTIME, I THINK I'LL GO TO BED. THANK YOU FOR YOUR INFORMATION, AND ENJOY THE REST OF THE EVENING.
TALK ABOUT A 10-FOOT WRENCH IN THE WORKS! I HAVE TO FIND SOME WAY TO CONTACT THIS ANGEL.
ONE MOMENT, SEÑOR.
WHERE DO YOU THINK YOU'RE GOING?
BUT... FOR SOME AIR IN THE PARK. IT'S SO STUFFY INSIDE.
25

ALLOW ME TO ACCOMPANY YOU, SEÑOR.
WHY? AREN'T THE PRESIDENTIAL GARDENS SAFE?
I WAS ORDERED TO LOOK AFTER YOU, AND I'M FOLLOWING MY ORDERS. THAT'S ALL.
YOU'RE RIGHT, CAPTAIN GARCIA. EVERYONE KNOWS THAT OBEDIENCE IS THE FIRST OF THE MILITARY VIRTUES.
WOULD YOU MIND IF I JOINED YOU? THE PERSON WHO DROVE ME HERE LEFT WITHOUT WAITING.
?
!
?
KARL MEREDITH, BUSINESSMAN. COULD YOU DROP ME OFF AT HOTEL CRISTOBAL?
WELL... ER... CERTAINLY... ER... WITH PLEASURE...
ARE YOU RELATED TO THE NEWCASTLE MEREDITHS, BY ANY CHANCE?
WE'RE ALMOST THERE. THE CRISTOBAL IS...
?!
TALLER PACO
TALLER PACO
?
?!
??

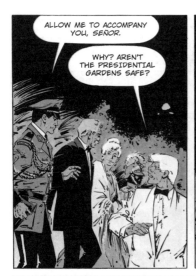

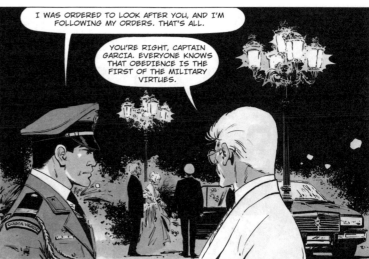

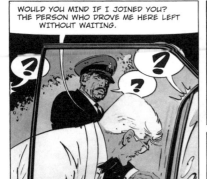

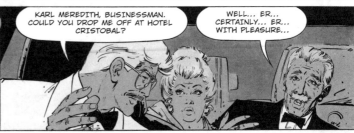

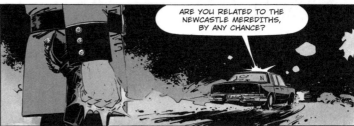

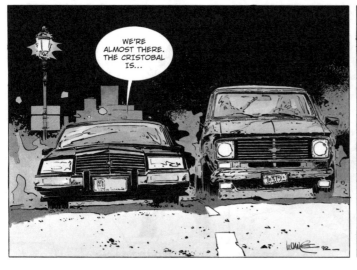

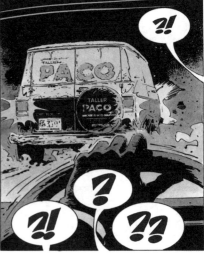

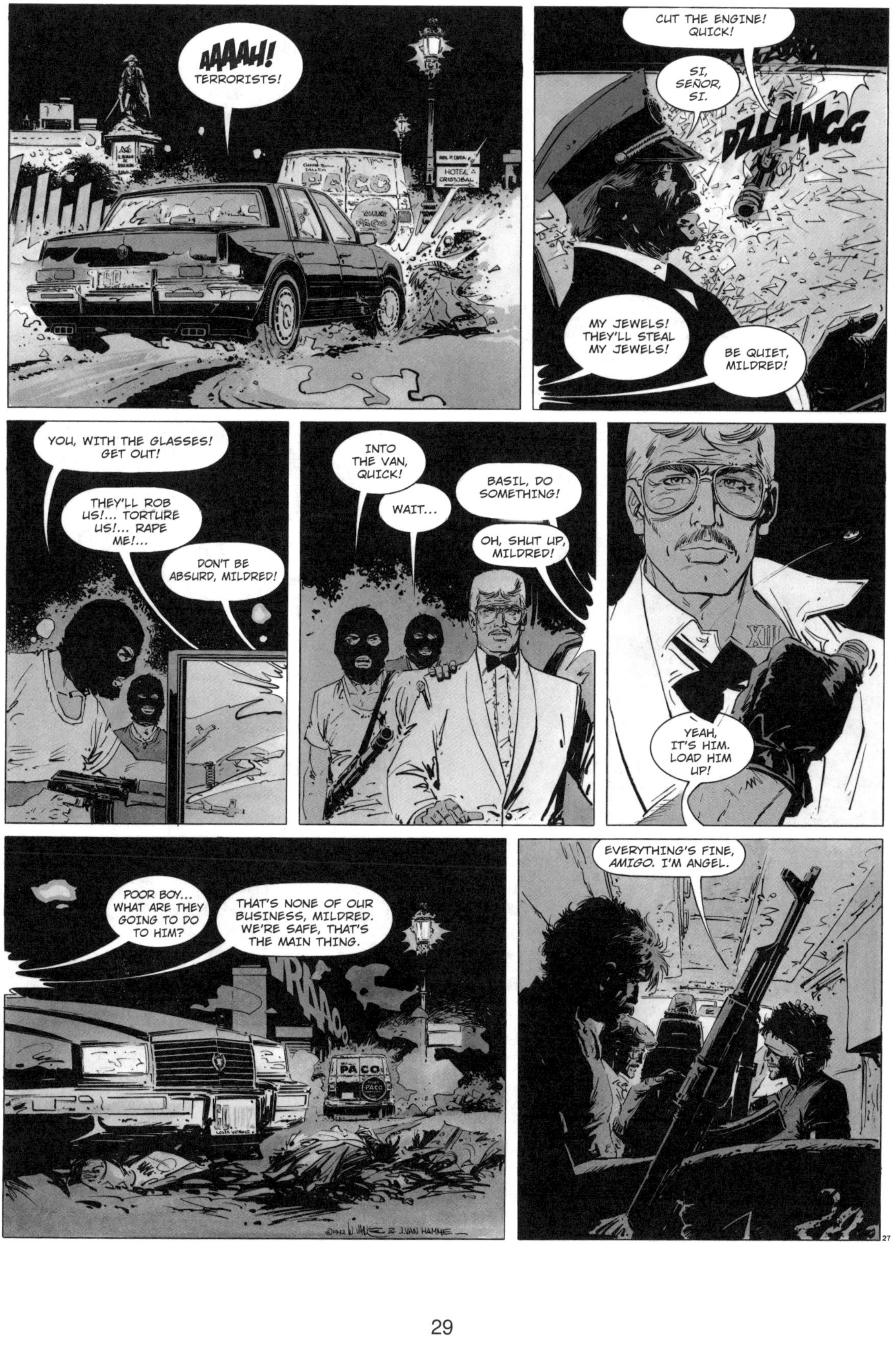
AAAAH! TERRORISTS!
CUT THE ENGINE! QUICK!
SI, SEÑOR, SI.
DZLAINGG
MY JEWELS! THEY'LL STEAL MY JEWELS!
BE QUIET, MILDRED!
YOU, WITH THE GLASSES! GET OUT!
THEY'LL ROB US!... TORTURE US!... RAPE ME!...
DON'T BE ABSURD, MILDRED!
INTO THE VAN, QUICK!
WAIT...
BASIL, DO SOMETHING!
OH, SHUT UP, MILDRED!
YEAH, IT'S HIM. LOAD HIM UP!
POOR BOY... WHAT ARE THEY GOING TO DO TO HIM?
THAT'S NONE OF OUR BUSINESS, MILDRED. WE'RE SAFE, THAT'S THE MAIN THING.
VRAAAOO
EVERYTHING'S FINE, AMIGO. I'M ANGEL.
W. VANCE & J. VAN HAMME
27

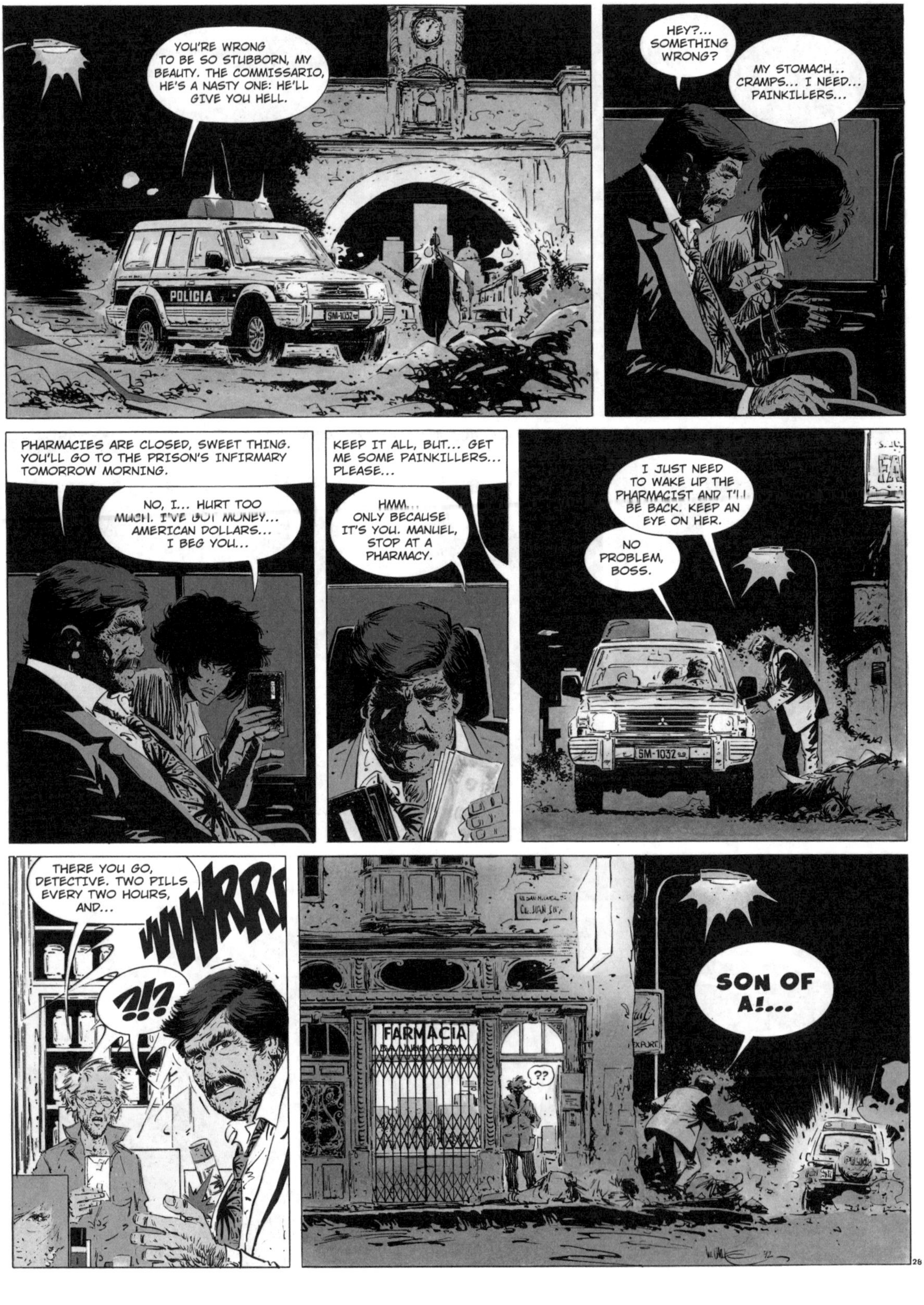
YOU'RE WRONG TO BE SO STUBBORN, MY BEAUTY. THE COMMISSARIO, HE'S A NASTY ONE: HE'LL GIVE YOU HELL.
POLICIA
HEY?... SOMETHING WRONG?
MY STOMACH... CRAMPS... I NEED... PAINKILLERS...
PHARMACIES ARE CLOSED, SWEET THING. YOU'LL GO TO THE PRISON'S INFIRMARY TOMORROW MORNING.
NO, I... HURT TOO MUCH. I'VE GOT MONEY... AMERICAN DOLLARS... I BEG YOU...
KEEP IT ALL, BUT... GET ME SOME PAINKILLERS... PLEASE...
HMM... ONLY BECAUSE IT'S YOU. MANUEL, STOP AT A PHARMACY.
I JUST NEED TO WAKE UP THE PHARMACIST AND I'LL BE BACK. KEEP AN EYE ON HER.
NO PROBLEM, BOSS.
THERE YOU GO, DETECTIVE. TWO PILLS EVERY TWO HOURS, AND...
WWRRR
?!?
FARMACIA
??
SON OF A!...
28

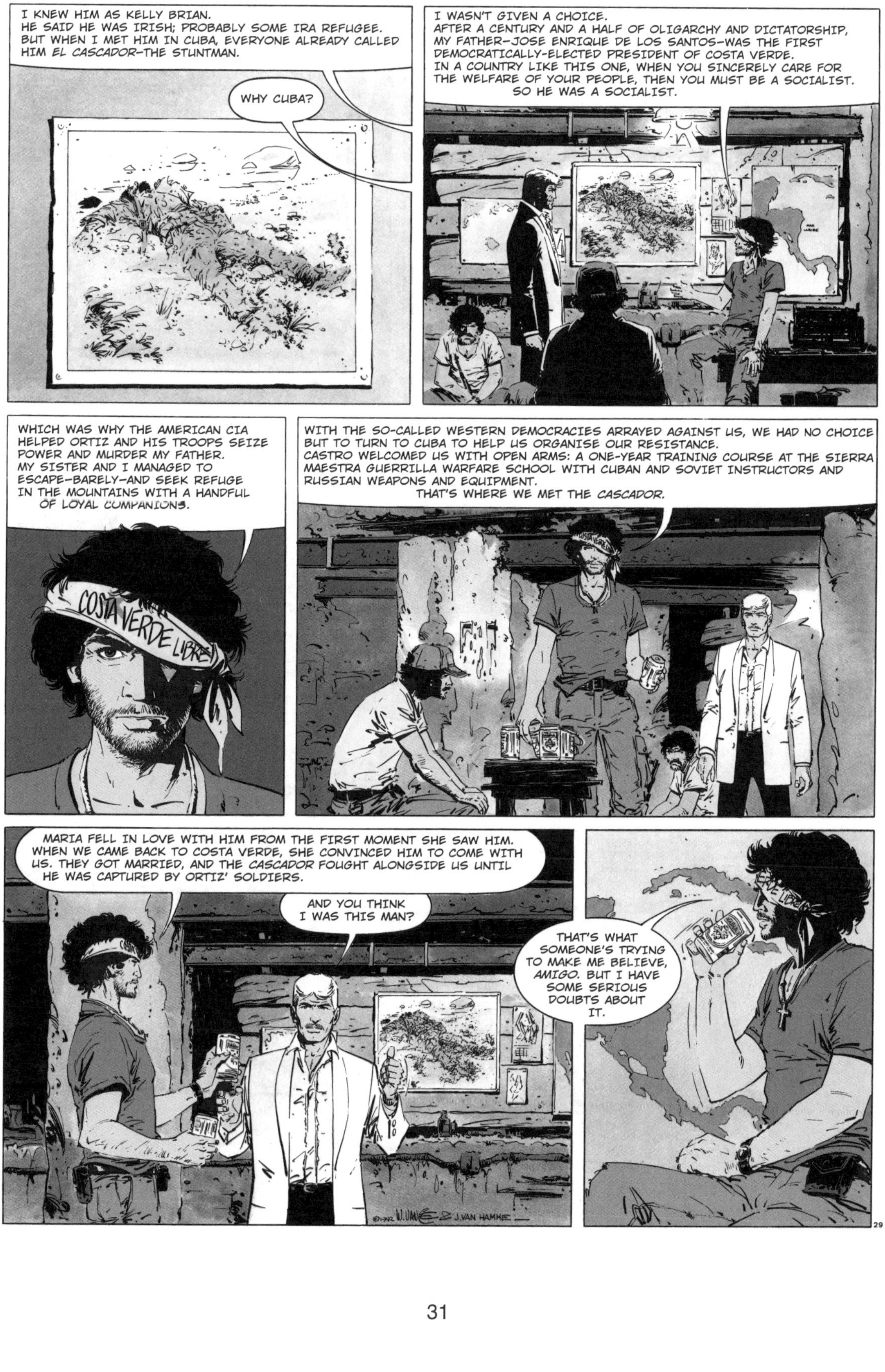
I KNEW HIM AS KELLY BRIAN.
HE SAID HE WAS IRISH; PROBABLY SOME IRA REFUGEE.
BUT WHEN I MET HIM IN CUBA, EVERYONE ALREADY CALLED HIM *EL CASCADOR*–THE STUNTMAN.
WHY CUBA?
I WASN'T GIVEN A CHOICE.
AFTER A CENTURY AND A HALF OF OLIGARCHY AND DICTATORSHIP, MY FATHER–JOSE ENRIQUE DE LOS SANTOS–WAS THE FIRST DEMOCRATICALLY-ELECTED PRESIDENT OF COSTA VERDE.
IN A COUNTRY LIKE THIS ONE, WHEN YOU SINCERELY CARE FOR THE WELFARE OF YOUR PEOPLE, THEN YOU MUST BE A SOCIALIST.
SO HE WAS A SOCIALIST.
WHICH WAS WHY THE AMERICAN CIA HELPED ORTIZ AND HIS TROOPS SEIZE POWER AND MURDER MY FATHER.
MY SISTER AND I MANAGED TO ESCAPE–BARELY–AND SEEK REFUGE IN THE MOUNTAINS WITH A HANDFUL OF LOYAL COMPANIONS.
COSTA VERDE LIBRE
WITH THE SO-CALLED WESTERN DEMOCRACIES ARRAYED AGAINST US, WE HAD NO CHOICE BUT TO TURN TO CUBA TO HELP US ORGANISE OUR RESISTANCE.
CASTRO WELCOMED US WITH OPEN ARMS: A ONE-YEAR TRAINING COURSE AT THE SIERRA MAESTRA GUERRILLA WARFARE SCHOOL WITH CUBAN AND SOVIET INSTRUCTORS AND RUSSIAN WEAPONS AND EQUIPMENT.
THAT'S WHERE WE MET THE *CASCADOR*.
MARIA FELL IN LOVE WITH HIM FROM THE FIRST MOMENT SHE SAW HIM. WHEN WE CAME BACK TO COSTA VERDE, SHE CONVINCED HIM TO COME WITH US. THEY GOT MARRIED, AND THE *CASCADOR* FOUGHT ALONGSIDE US UNTIL HE WAS CAPTURED BY ORTIZ' SOLDIERS.
AND YOU THINK I WAS THIS MAN?
THAT'S WHAT SOMEONE'S TRYING TO MAKE ME BELIEVE, *AMIGO*. BUT I HAVE SOME SERIOUS DOUBTS ABOUT IT.
J. VAN HAMME
29

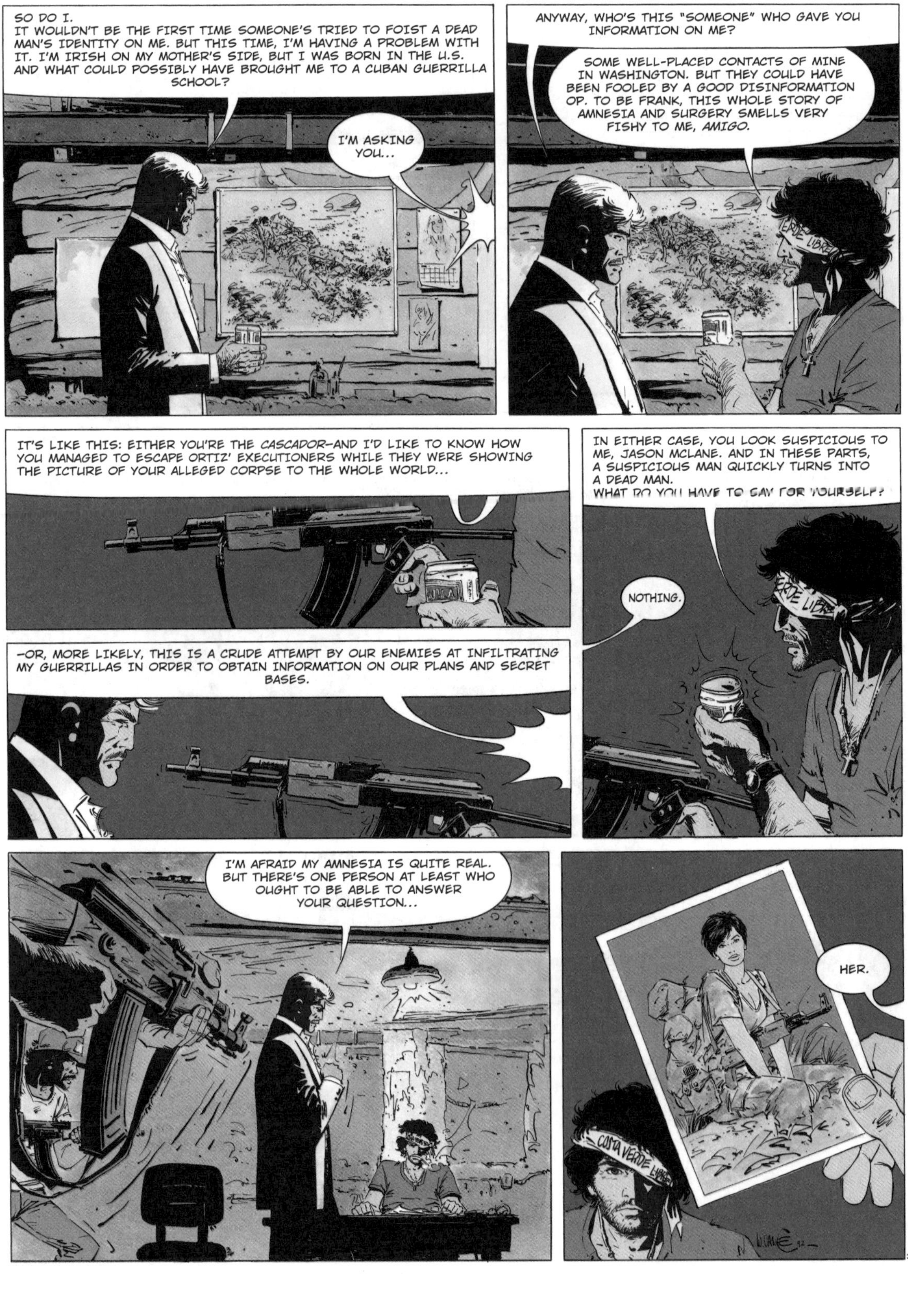
SO DO I.
IT WOULDN'T BE THE FIRST TIME SOMEONE'S TRIED TO FOIST A DEAD MAN'S IDENTITY ON ME. BUT THIS TIME, I'M HAVING A PROBLEM WITH IT. I'M IRISH ON MY MOTHER'S SIDE, BUT I WAS BORN IN THE U.S. AND WHAT COULD POSSIBLY HAVE BROUGHT ME TO A CUBAN GUERRILLA SCHOOL?
I'M ASKING YOU...
ANYWAY, WHO'S THIS "SOMEONE" WHO GAVE YOU INFORMATION ON ME?
SOME WELL-PLACED CONTACTS OF MINE IN WASHINGTON. BUT THEY COULD HAVE BEEN FOOLED BY A GOOD DISINFORMATION OP. TO BE FRANK, THIS WHOLE STORY OF AMNESIA AND SURGERY SMELLS VERY FISHY TO ME, *AMIGO*.
IT'S LIKE THIS: EITHER YOU'RE THE *CASCADOR*–AND I'D LIKE TO KNOW HOW YOU MANAGED TO ESCAPE ORTIZ' EXECUTIONERS WHILE THEY WERE SHOWING THE PICTURE OF YOUR ALLEGED CORPSE TO THE WHOLE WORLD...
–OR, MORE LIKELY, THIS IS A CRUDE ATTEMPT BY OUR ENEMIES AT INFILTRATING MY GUERRILLAS IN ORDER TO OBTAIN INFORMATION ON OUR PLANS AND SECRET BASES.
IN EITHER CASE, YOU LOOK SUSPICIOUS TO ME, JASON MCLANE. AND IN THESE PARTS, A SUSPICIOUS MAN QUICKLY TURNS INTO A DEAD MAN.
WHAT DO YOU HAVE TO SAY FOR YOURSELF?
NOTHING.
I'M AFRAID MY AMNESIA IS QUITE REAL. BUT THERE'S ONE PERSON AT LEAST WHO OUGHT TO BE ABLE TO ANSWER YOUR QUESTION...
HER.
COSTA VERDE LIBRE
30

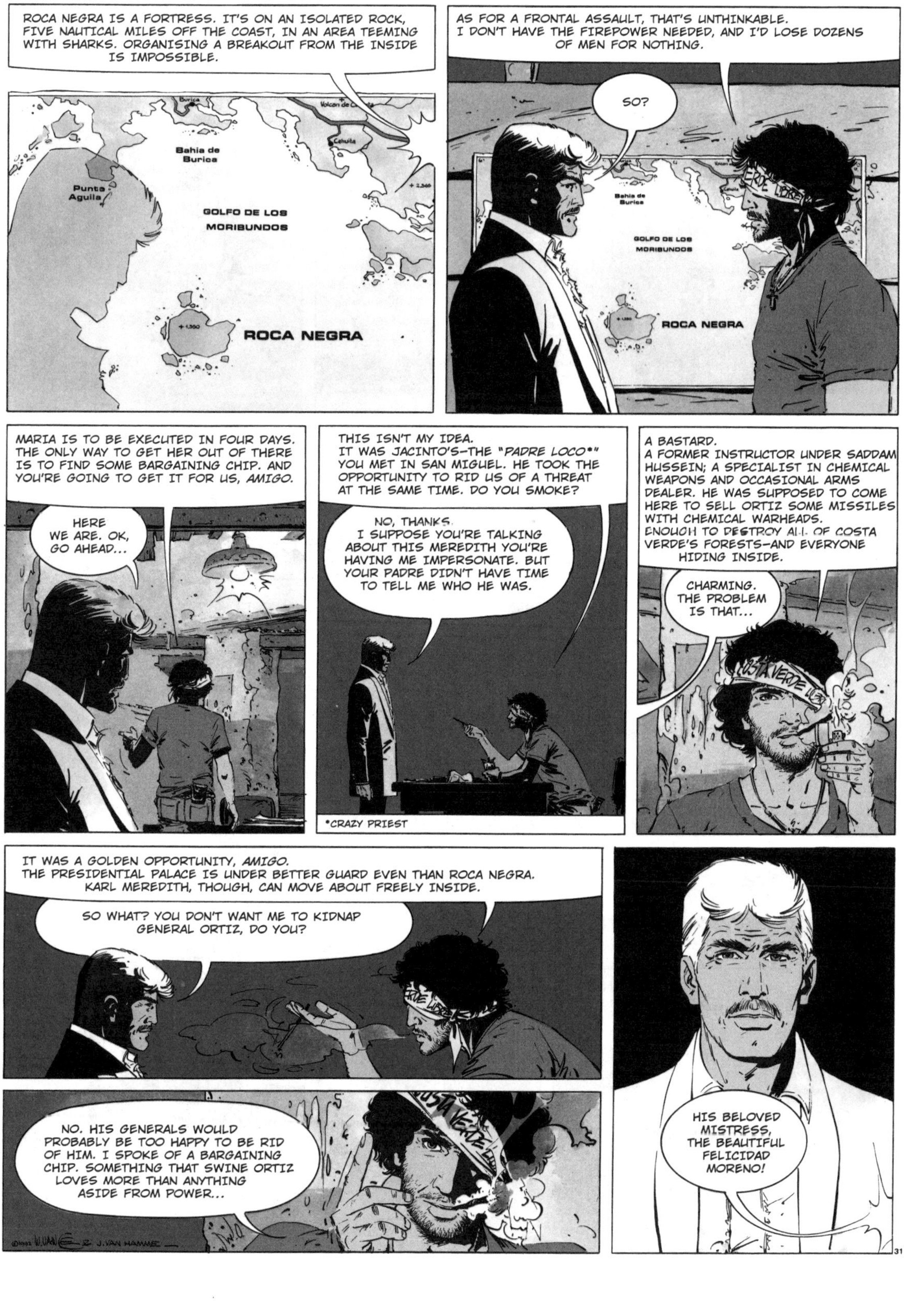
ROCA NEGRA IS A FORTRESS. IT'S ON AN ISOLATED ROCK, FIVE NAUTICAL MILES OFF THE COAST, IN AN AREA TEEMING WITH SHARKS. ORGANISING A BREAKOUT FROM THE INSIDE IS IMPOSSIBLE.
Burica
Bahia de Burica
Cahuila
Punta Aguila
GOLFO DE LOS MORIBUNDOS
ROCA NEGRA
AS FOR A FRONTAL ASSAULT, THAT'S UNTHINKABLE. I DON'T HAVE THE FIREPOWER NEEDED, AND I'D LOSE DOZENS OF MEN FOR NOTHING.
SO?
MARIA IS TO BE EXECUTED IN FOUR DAYS. THE ONLY WAY TO GET HER OUT OF THERE IS TO FIND SOME BARGAINING CHIP. AND YOU'RE GOING TO GET IT FOR US, *AMIGO*.
HERE WE ARE. OK, GO AHEAD...
THIS ISN'T MY IDEA. IT WAS JACINTO'S–THE "*PADRE LOCO**" YOU MET IN SAN MIGUEL. HE TOOK THE OPPORTUNITY TO RID US OF A THREAT AT THE SAME TIME. DO YOU SMOKE?
NO, THANKS. I SUPPOSE YOU'RE TALKING ABOUT THIS MEREDITH YOU'RE HAVING ME IMPERSONATE. BUT YOUR PADRE DIDN'T HAVE TIME TO TELL ME WHO HE WAS.
*CRAZY PRIEST
A BASTARD. A FORMER INSTRUCTOR UNDER SADDAM HUSSEIN; A SPECIALIST IN CHEMICAL WEAPONS AND OCCASIONAL ARMS DEALER. HE WAS SUPPOSED TO COME HERE TO SELL ORTIZ SOME MISSILES WITH CHEMICAL WARHEADS. ENOUGH TO DESTROY ALL OF COSTA VERDE'S FORESTS–AND EVERYONE HIDING INSIDE.
CHARMING. THE PROBLEM IS THAT...
COSTA VERDE
IT WAS A GOLDEN OPPORTUNITY, *AMIGO*. THE PRESIDENTIAL PALACE IS UNDER BETTER GUARD EVEN THAN ROCA NEGRA. KARL MEREDITH, THOUGH, CAN MOVE ABOUT FREELY INSIDE.
SO WHAT? YOU DON'T WANT ME TO KIDNAP GENERAL ORTIZ, DO YOU?
NO. HIS GENERALS WOULD PROBABLY BE TOO HAPPY TO BE RID OF HIM. I SPOKE OF A BARGAINING CHIP. SOMETHING THAT SWINE ORTIZ LOVES MORE THAN ANYTHING ASIDE FROM POWER...
HIS BELOVED MISTRESS, THE BEAUTIFUL FELICIDAD MORENO!
J. VAN HAMME
31

SHE'S REALLY AN AMERICAN. FELICITY BROWN*, WIDOW OF A SMALL LANDOWNER FROM THE SOUTHERN UNITED STATES. IT SEEMS THAT BEFORE BEING COVERED IN GOLD IN ORTIZ' BED, SHE HAD SOME TROUBLE WITH HER COUNTRY'S COURTS.

I KNOW ALL THAT, ANGEL.

* BROWN: MORENO IN SPANISH

IT SO HAPPENS THAT I KNOW HER. AND SHE HAS LITTLE REASON TO LIKE ME**. IT'S OUT OF THE QUESTION FOR ME TO GO BACK TO THE PALACE.

IT'S A BUMMER, BUT IT CHANGES NOTHING, AMIGO. YOU DON'T HAVE A CHOICE.

**SEE WHERE THE INDIAN WALKS.

IF YOU'RE A TRAITOR AND TRY TO LEAVE THE COUNTRY, I CAN ASSURE YOU YOU'LL NEVER REACH THE BORDER ALIVE. ON THE OTHER HAND, IF YOU'RE REALLY AMNESIC, YOU'LL WANT TO KNOW. AND MORENO IS OUR BEST CHANCE TO SAVE MARIA.

AND HOW DO YOU THINK I SHOULD GO ABOUT IT?

THAT'S YOUR PROBLEM. MY INFORMANTS ASSURED ME THAT JASON MOLAND, WHETHER HE REALLY IS THE CASCADOR OR NOT, IS CAPABLE OF GETTING OUT OF JUST ABOUT ANY SITUATION. NOW'S THE TIME TO PROVE IT.

BECAUSE IF MARIA DIES, I SWEAR ON MY FATHER'S HEAD THAT YOU WILL DIE TOO, NO MATTER WHERE YOU HIDE!

VERY SCARY. BUT YOU'RE RIGHT ABOUT ONE THING, JORGE DE LOS SANTOS: I WANT TO KNOW. SO, MIGHT AS WELL GIVE IT A TRY.

GOOD. MORENO NEVER LEAVES THE PALACE WITHOUT A STRONG ESCORT. YOU'LL HAVE TO ACT FROM THE INSIDE, AND QUICKLY. WHETHER SHE RECOGNISES YOU OR NOT, IT WON'T TAKE PERALTA FOUR DAYS TO DISCOVER YOU'RE NOT MEREDITH. WATCH OUT FOR HIM; HE WAS THE ONE WHO CAPTURED THE CASCADOR AND HAD HIM EXECUTED THREE YEARS AGO.

FOR THE NEXT THREE DAYS, JOAQUIN WILL WAIT FOR YOU FROM MIDNIGHT ON AT THE *MUELLE DE LA VIRGEN*, AT THE WESTERN SIDE OF THE HARBOUR. HE'LL HAVE A FAST BOAT READY. QUESTIONS?

JUST ONE...

*PIER OF THE VIRGIN

HOW AM I GOING TO RETURN TO THE PALACE WITHOUT ATTRACTING SUSPICION?

A SIMPLE MATTER OF APPEARANCES, AMIGO.

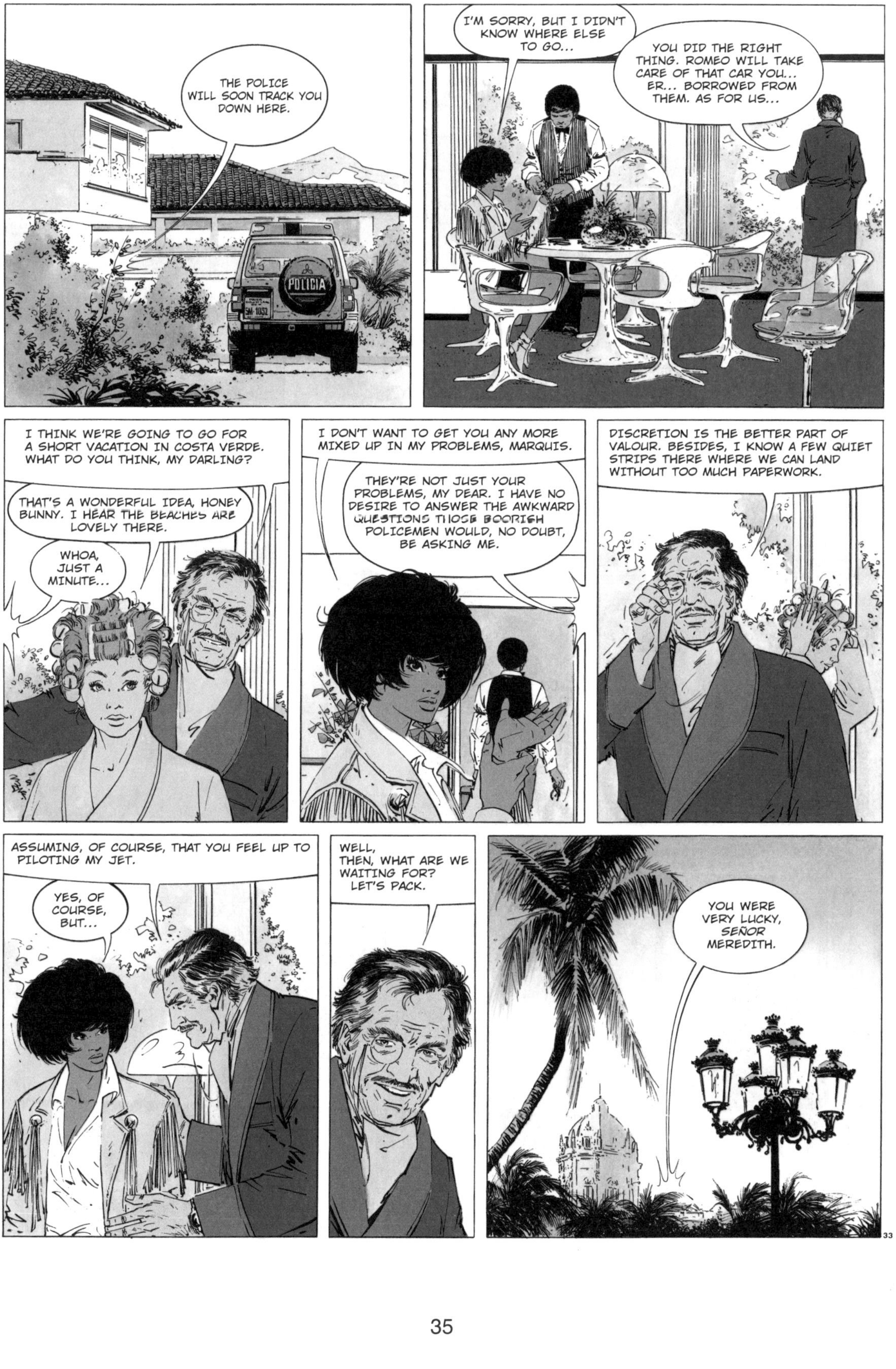
THE POLICE WILL SOON TRACK YOU DOWN HERE.
I'M SORRY, BUT I DIDN'T KNOW WHERE ELSE TO GO...
YOU DID THE RIGHT THING. ROMEO WILL TAKE CARE OF THAT CAR YOU... ER... BORROWED FROM THEM. AS FOR US...
I THINK WE'RE GOING TO GO FOR A SHORT VACATION IN COSTA VERDE. WHAT DO YOU THINK, MY DARLING?
THAT'S A WONDERFUL IDEA, HONEY BUNNY. I HEAR THE BEACHES ARE LOVELY THERE.
WHOA, JUST A MINUTE...
I DON'T WANT TO GET YOU ANY MORE MIXED UP IN MY PROBLEMS, MARQUIS.
THEY'RE NOT JUST YOUR PROBLEMS, MY DEAR. I HAVE NO DESIRE TO ANSWER THE AWKWARD QUESTIONS THOSE BOORISH POLICEMEN WOULD, NO DOUBT, BE ASKING ME.
DISCRETION IS THE BETTER PART OF VALOUR. BESIDES, I KNOW A FEW QUIET STRIPS THERE WHERE WE CAN LAND WITHOUT TOO MUCH PAPERWORK.
ASSUMING, OF COURSE, THAT YOU FEEL UP TO PILOTING MY JET.
YES, OF COURSE, BUT...
WELL, THEN, WHAT ARE WE WAITING FOR? LET'S PACK.
YOU WERE VERY LUCKY, SEÑOR MEREDITH.
33

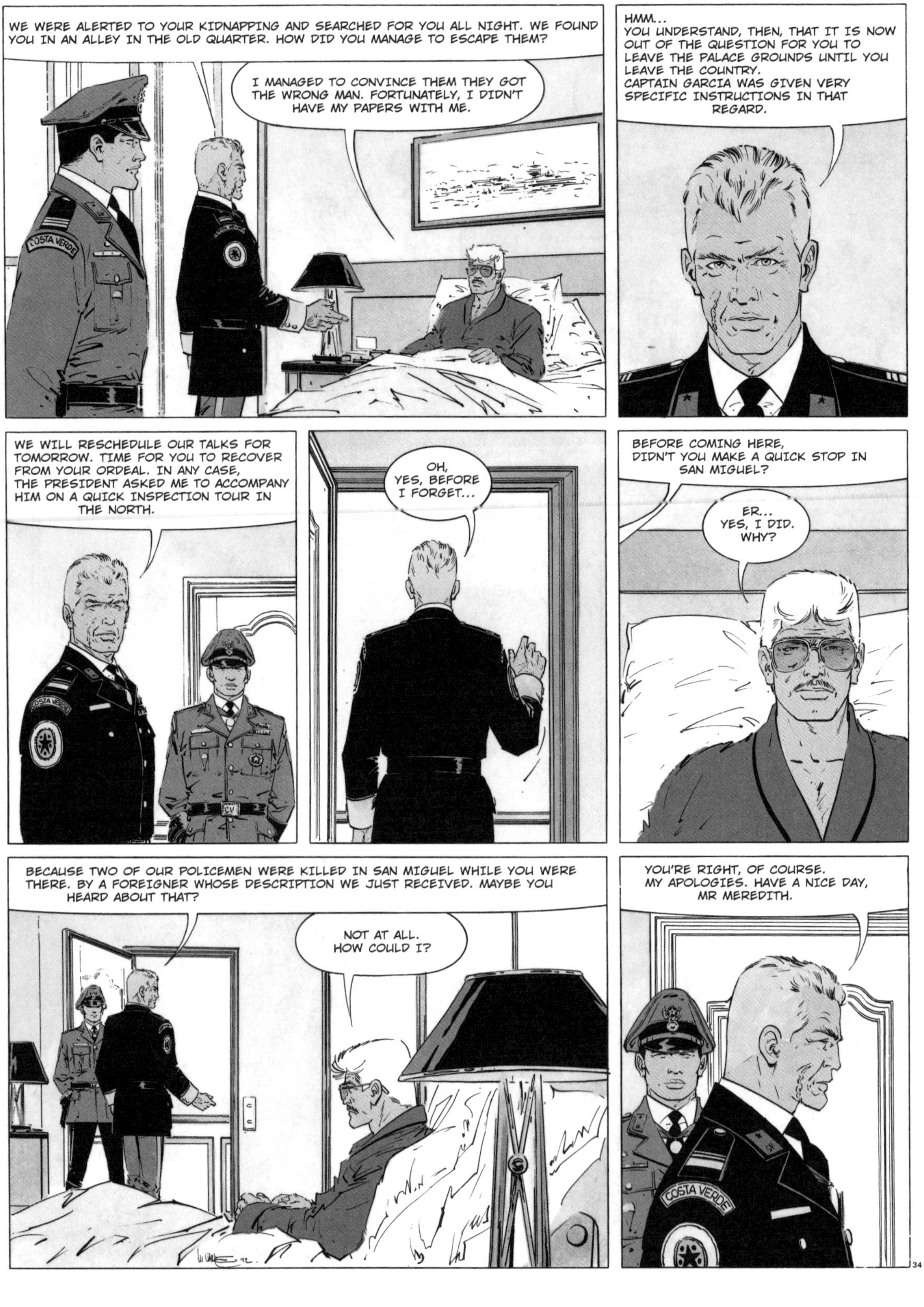
WE WERE ALERTED TO YOUR KIDNAPPING AND SEARCHED FOR YOU ALL NIGHT. WE FOUND YOU IN AN ALLEY IN THE OLD QUARTER. HOW DID YOU MANAGE TO ESCAPE THEM?
I MANAGED TO CONVINCE THEM THEY GOT THE WRONG MAN. FORTUNATELY, I DIDN'T HAVE MY PAPERS WITH ME.
COSTA VERDE
HMM... YOU UNDERSTAND, THEN, THAT IT IS NOW OUT OF THE QUESTION FOR YOU TO LEAVE THE PALACE GROUNDS UNTIL YOU LEAVE THE COUNTRY. CAPTAIN GARCIA WAS GIVEN VERY SPECIFIC INSTRUCTIONS IN THAT REGARD.
WE WILL RESCHEDULE OUR TALKS FOR TOMORROW. TIME FOR YOU TO RECOVER FROM YOUR ORDEAL. IN ANY CASE, THE PRESIDENT ASKED ME TO ACCOMPANY HIM ON A QUICK INSPECTION TOUR IN THE NORTH.
COSTA VERDE
CV
OH, YES, BEFORE I FORGET...
BEFORE COMING HERE, DIDN'T YOU MAKE A QUICK STOP IN SAN MIGUEL?
ER... YES, I DID. WHY?
BECAUSE TWO OF OUR POLICEMEN WERE KILLED IN SAN MIGUEL WHILE YOU WERE THERE. BY A FOREIGNER WHOSE DESCRIPTION WE JUST RECEIVED. MAYBE YOU HEARD ABOUT THAT?
NOT AT ALL. HOW COULD I?
YOU'RE RIGHT, OF COURSE. MY APOLOGIES. HAVE A NICE DAY, MR MEREDITH.
COSTA VERDE
34

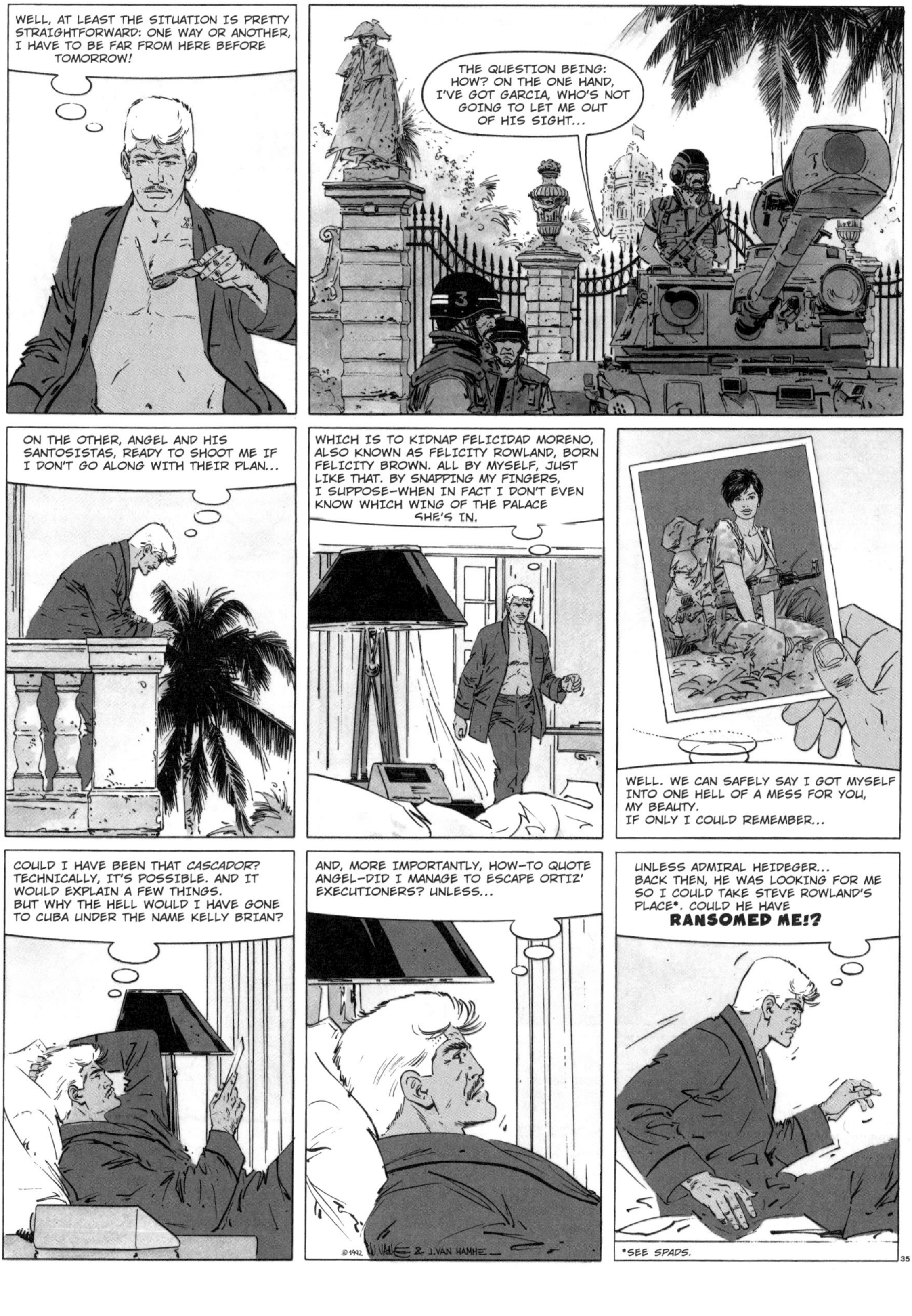
WELL, AT LEAST THE SITUATION IS PRETTY STRAIGHTFORWARD: ONE WAY OR ANOTHER, I HAVE TO BE FAR FROM HERE BEFORE TOMORROW!
THE QUESTION BEING: HOW? ON THE ONE HAND, I'VE GOT GARCIA, WHO'S NOT GOING TO LET ME OUT OF HIS SIGHT...
ON THE OTHER, ANGEL AND HIS SANTOSISTAS, READY TO SHOOT ME IF I DON'T GO ALONG WITH THEIR PLAN...
WHICH IS TO KIDNAP FELICIDAD MORENO, ALSO KNOWN AS FELICITY ROWLAND, BORN FELICITY BROWN. ALL BY MYSELF, JUST LIKE THAT. BY SNAPPING MY FINGERS, I SUPPOSE–WHEN IN FACT I DON'T EVEN KNOW WHICH WING OF THE PALACE SHE'S IN.
WELL. WE CAN SAFELY SAY I GOT MYSELF INTO ONE HELL OF A MESS FOR YOU, MY BEAUTY. IF ONLY I COULD REMEMBER...
COULD I HAVE BEEN THAT CASCADOR? TECHNICALLY, IT'S POSSIBLE. AND IT WOULD EXPLAIN A FEW THINGS. BUT WHY THE HELL WOULD I HAVE GONE TO CUBA UNDER THE NAME KELLY BRIAN?
AND, MORE IMPORTANTLY, HOW–TO QUOTE ANGEL–DID I MANAGE TO ESCAPE ORTIZ' EXECUTIONERS? UNLESS...
UNLESS ADMIRAL HEIDEGER... BACK THEN, HE WAS LOOKING FOR ME SO I COULD TAKE STEVE ROWLAND'S PLACE*. COULD HE HAVE RANSOMED ME!?
©1992 W. VANCE & J. VAN HAMME
*SEE SPADS.
35

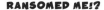

OF COURSE: PERALTA!
THE MAN WHO CAPTURED THE CASCADOR!
HE KNOWS THE TRUTH TOO. PROBLEM IS,
I CAN'T REALLY SEE MYSELF ASKING HIM
ABOUT IT...

YOUR BREAKFAST, SEÑOR.

YOU HAVEN'T UNPACKED YOUR LUGGAGE YET?

IF YOU WANT TO CHECK THAT I HAVEN'T HIDDEN A WEAPON INSIDE, GO RIGHT AHEAD, CAPTAIN.

OUR SECURITY TEAMS HAVE ALREADY MADE SURE OF THAT, SEÑOR.
BUT DON'T YOU WORRY. THEY HAVEN'T TOUCHED YOUR PRECIOUS CATALOGUES.

?

MUSTARD GAS WARHEADS, CHLORINE ROCKETS, DEFOLIANT BOMBS, CYANHYDRIC ACID, VESICANT GRENADES. IT'S ALL THERE...

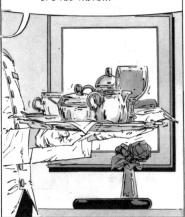

DO YOU DISAPPROVE OF YOUR SUPERIORS' CHOICES, CAPTAIN GARCIA?

I'M A SOLDIER, SEÑOR. I DEAL DEATH WHEN I'M ORDERED.

BUT THERE ARE WAYS TO KILL, AND THEN THERE ARE WAYS TO KILL. I DON'T EXPECT A MAN LIKE YOU TO UNDERSTAND. BUT THAT'S NOT WHY I CAME.

LA SEÑORITA MORENO, THE PRESIDENT'S PERSONAL ADVISOR, WOULD LIKE YOU TO DINE WITH HER TONIGHT, AT 2100 HOURS SHARP.

?!?

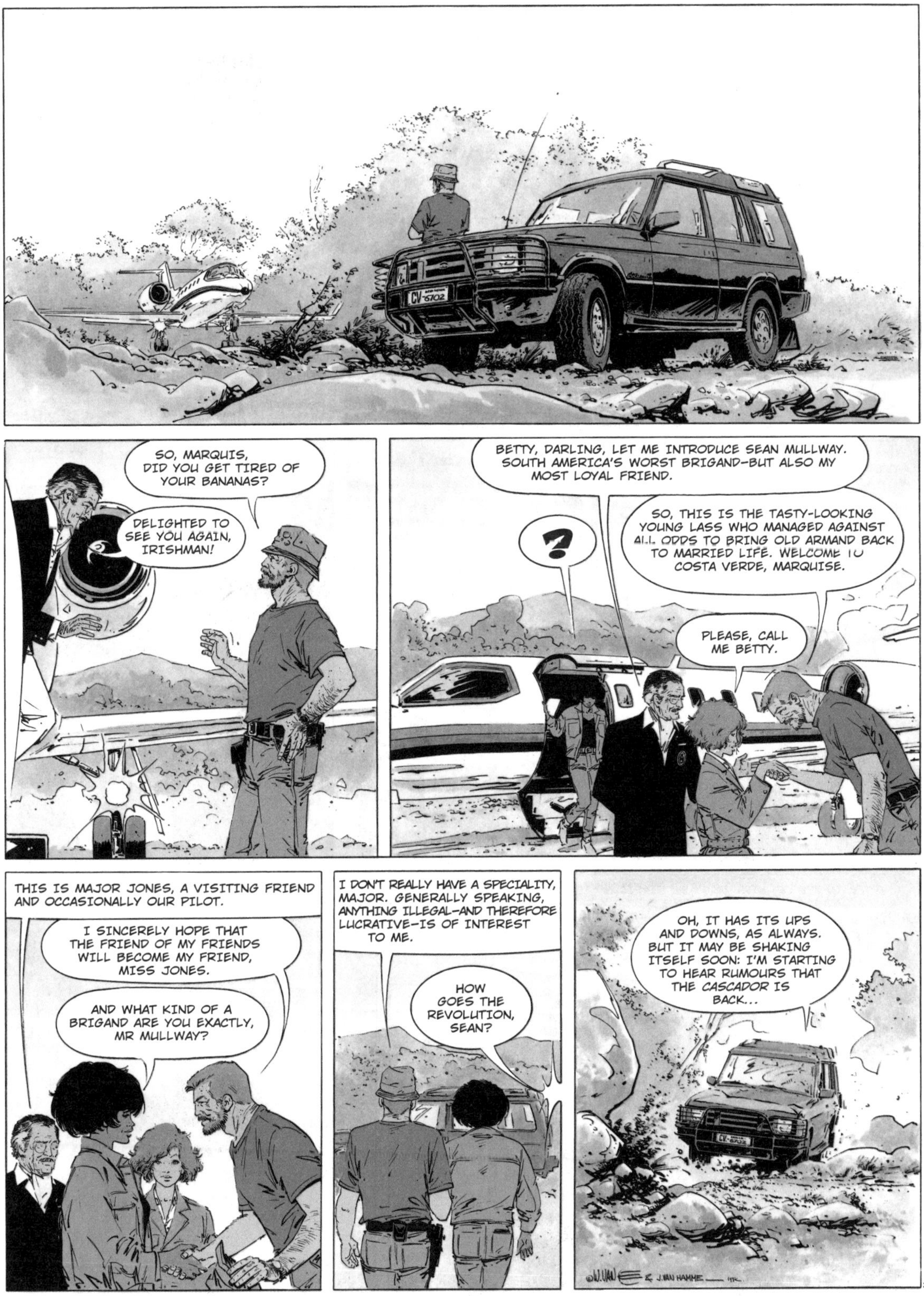
SO, MARQUIS, DID YOU GET TIRED OF YOUR BANANAS?
DELIGHTED TO SEE YOU AGAIN, IRISHMAN!
BETTY, DARLING, LET ME INTRODUCE SEAN MULLWAY. SOUTH AMERICA'S WORST BRIGAND—BUT ALSO MY MOST LOYAL FRIEND.
?
SO, THIS IS THE TASTY-LOOKING YOUNG LASS WHO MANAGED AGAINST ALL ODDS TO BRING OLD ARMAND BACK TO MARRIED LIFE. WELCOME TO COSTA VERDE, MARQUISE.
PLEASE, CALL ME BETTY.
THIS IS MAJOR JONES, A VISITING FRIEND AND OCCASIONALLY OUR PILOT.
I SINCERELY HOPE THAT THE FRIEND OF MY FRIENDS WILL BECOME MY FRIEND, MISS JONES.
AND WHAT KIND OF A BRIGAND ARE YOU EXACTLY, MR MULLWAY?
I DON'T REALLY HAVE A SPECIALITY, MAJOR. GENERALLY SPEAKING, ANYTHING ILLEGAL—AND THEREFORE LUCRATIVE—IS OF INTEREST TO ME.
HOW GOES THE REVOLUTION, SEAN?
OH, IT HAS ITS UPS AND DOWNS, AS ALWAYS. BUT IT MAY BE SHAKING ITSELF SOON: I'M STARTING TO HEAR RUMOURS THAT THE *CASCADOR* IS BACK...
J. VAN HAMME

37

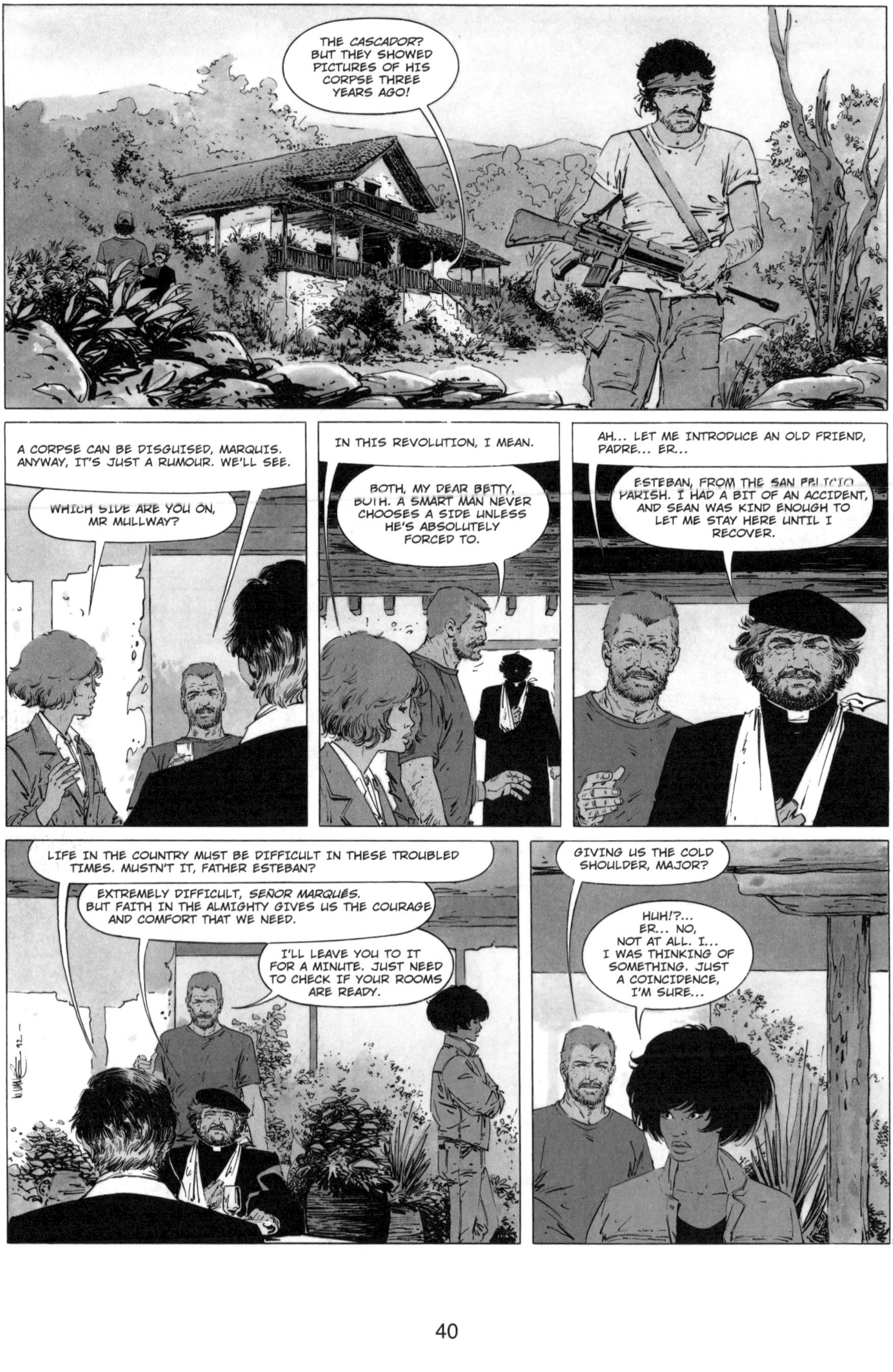
THE *CASCADOR*? BUT THEY SHOWED PICTURES OF HIS CORPSE THREE YEARS AGO!
A CORPSE CAN BE DISGUISED, MARQUIS. ANYWAY, IT'S JUST A RUMOUR. WE'LL SEE.
WHICH SIDE ARE YOU ON, MR MULLWAY?
IN THIS REVOLUTION, I MEAN.
BOTH, MY DEAR BETTY, BOTH. A SMART MAN NEVER CHOOSES A SIDE UNLESS HE'S ABSOLUTELY FORCED TO.
AH... LET ME INTRODUCE AN OLD FRIEND, PADRE... ER...
ESTEBAN, FROM THE SAN FELICIO PARISH. I HAD A BIT OF AN ACCIDENT, AND SEAN WAS KIND ENOUGH TO LET ME STAY HERE UNTIL I RECOVER.
LIFE IN THE COUNTRY MUST BE DIFFICULT IN THESE TROUBLED TIMES. MUSTN'T IT, FATHER ESTEBAN?
EXTREMELY DIFFICULT, *SEÑOR MARQUÉS*. BUT FAITH IN THE ALMIGHTY GIVES US THE COURAGE AND COMFORT THAT WE NEED.
I'LL LEAVE YOU TO IT FOR A MINUTE. JUST NEED TO CHECK IF YOUR ROOMS ARE READY.
GIVING US THE COLD SHOULDER, MAJOR?
HUH!?... ER... NO, NOT AT ALL. I... I WAS THINKING OF SOMETHING. JUST A COINCIDENCE, I'M SURE...
38

THE MOTHER OF ONE OF MY FRIENDS WAS CALLED MULLWAY.
MARGARET MULLWAY. SHE DIED IN NEW YORK SOME 30 YEARS AGO GIVING BIRTH TO HIM.
AND I WAS WONDERING...

MULLWAY IS A RATHER COMMON IRISH NAME, LASS.

BUT IT SO HAPPENS THAT I DID HAVE A SISTER NAMED MARGARET WHO DIED IN NEW YORK 31 YEARS AGO.
I DOUBT IT COULD HAVE BEEN THE SAME PERSON, THOUGH.

WHY?

MY SISTER DIED OF INFECTIOUS GASTROENTERITIS THAT WENT BAD.
SHE WASN'T MARRIED. AND, TO MY KNOWLEDGE, NEVER HAD ANY CHILDREN.

??

MAJOR?...

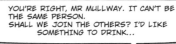

YOU'RE RIGHT, MR MULLWAY. IT CAN'T BE THE SAME PERSON.
SHALL WE JOIN THE OTHERS? I'D LIKE SOMETHING TO DRINK...

COME IN, MR MEREDITH, COME IN.
I CONGRATULATE YOU ON YOUR PUNCTUALITY.

YOU MAY LEAVE, CAPTAIN. BUT DON'T GO TOO FAR;
I MAY HAVE NEED OF YOU.

AS YOU WISH, SEÑORITA.

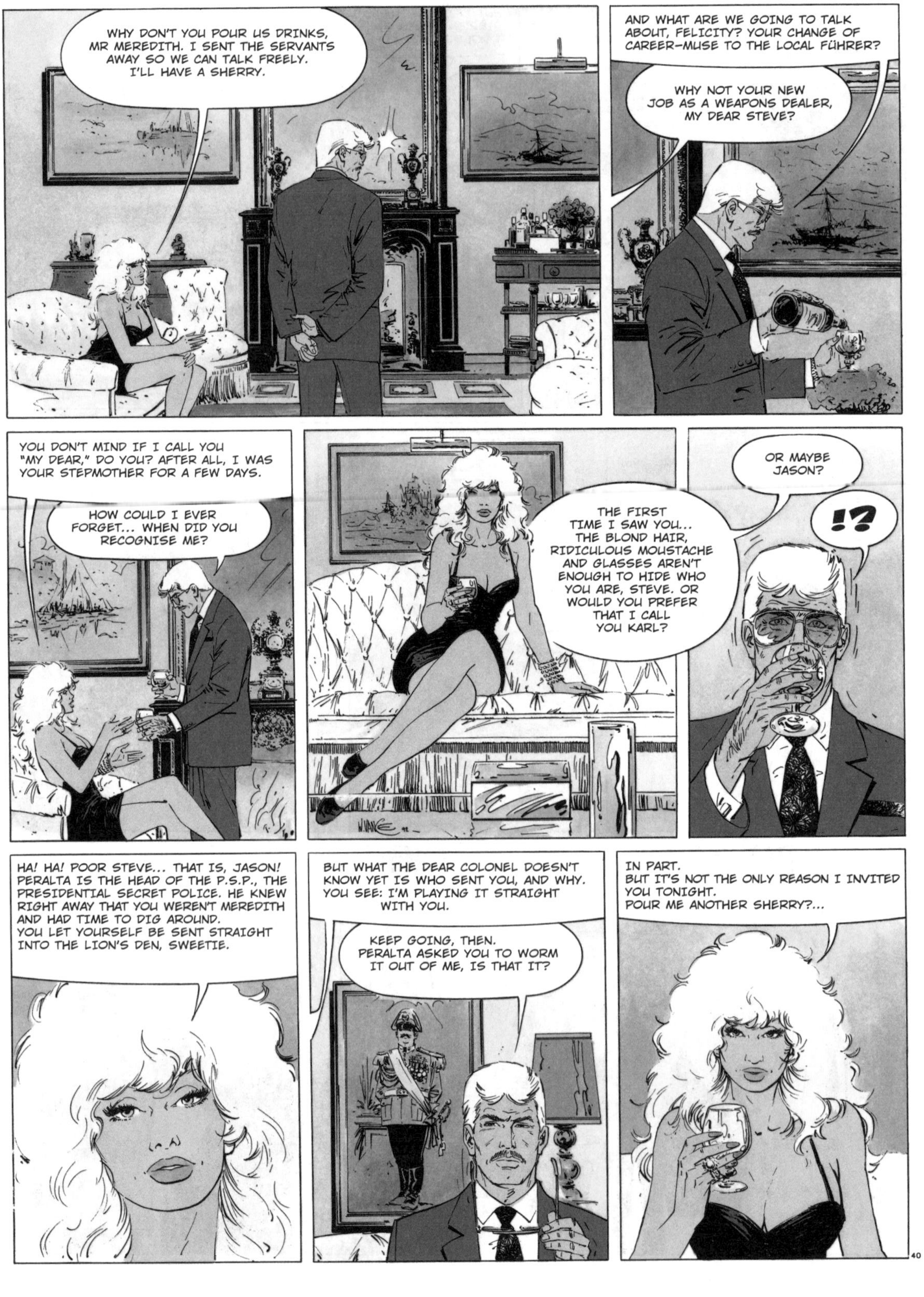
WHY DON'T YOU POUR US DRINKS, MR MEREDITH. I SENT THE SERVANTS AWAY SO WE CAN TALK FREELY. I'LL HAVE A SHERRY.
AND WHAT ARE WE GOING TO TALK ABOUT, FELICITY? YOUR CHANGE OF CAREER–MUSE TO THE LOCAL FÜHRER?
WHY NOT YOUR NEW JOB AS A WEAPONS DEALER, MY DEAR STEVE?
YOU DON'T MIND IF I CALL YOU "MY DEAR," DO YOU? AFTER ALL, I WAS YOUR STEPMOTHER FOR A FEW DAYS.
HOW COULD I EVER FORGET... WHEN DID YOU RECOGNISE ME?
THE FIRST TIME I SAW YOU... THE BLOND HAIR, RIDICULOUS MOUSTACHE AND GLASSES AREN'T ENOUGH TO HIDE WHO YOU ARE, STEVE. OR WOULD YOU PREFER THAT I CALL YOU KARL?
OR MAYBE JASON?
!?
HA! HA! POOR STEVE... THAT IS, JASON! PERALTA IS THE HEAD OF THE P.S.P., THE PRESIDENTIAL SECRET POLICE. HE KNEW RIGHT AWAY THAT YOU WEREN'T MEREDITH AND HAD TIME TO DIG AROUND. YOU LET YOURSELF BE SENT STRAIGHT INTO THE LION'S DEN, SWEETIE.
BUT WHAT THE DEAR COLONEL DOESN'T KNOW YET IS WHO SENT YOU, AND WHY. YOU SEE: I'M PLAYING IT STRAIGHT WITH YOU.
KEEP GOING, THEN. PERALTA ASKED YOU TO WORM IT OUT OF ME, IS THAT IT?
IN PART. BUT IT'S NOT THE ONLY REASON I INVITED YOU TONIGHT. POUR ME ANOTHER SHERRY?...
40

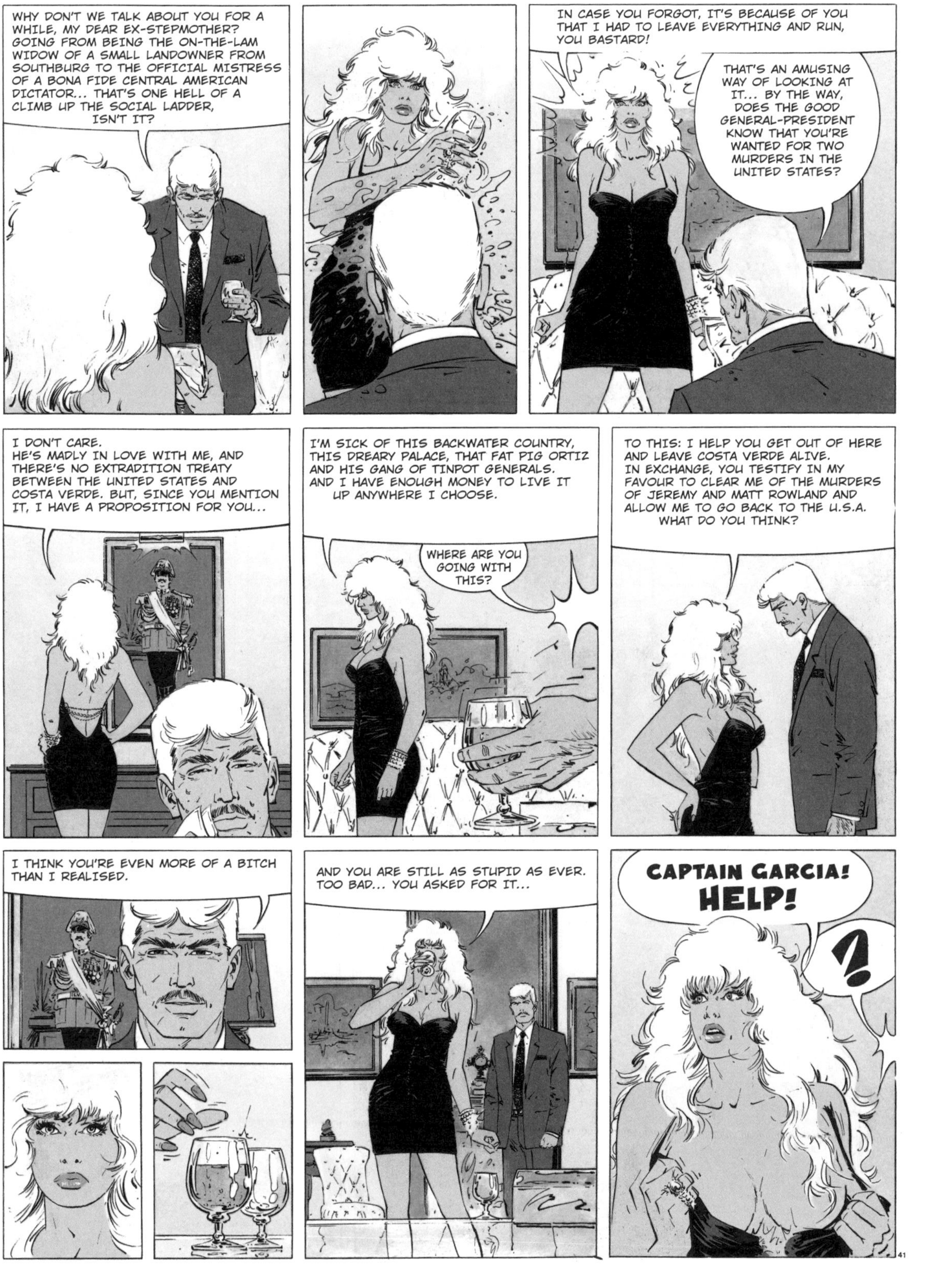
WHY DON'T WE TALK ABOUT YOU FOR A WHILE, MY DEAR EX-STEPMOTHER? GOING FROM BEING THE ON-THE-LAM WIDOW OF A SMALL LANDOWNER FROM SOUTHBURG TO THE OFFICIAL MISTRESS OF A BONA FIDE CENTRAL AMERICAN DICTATOR... THAT'S ONE HELL OF A CLIMB UP THE SOCIAL LADDER, ISN'T IT?
IN CASE YOU FORGOT, IT'S BECAUSE OF YOU THAT I HAD TO LEAVE EVERYTHING AND RUN, YOU BASTARD!
THAT'S AN AMUSING WAY OF LOOKING AT IT... BY THE WAY, DOES THE GOOD GENERAL-PRESIDENT KNOW THAT YOU'RE WANTED FOR TWO MURDERS IN THE UNITED STATES?
I DON'T CARE. HE'S MADLY IN LOVE WITH ME, AND THERE'S NO EXTRADITION TREATY BETWEEN THE UNITED STATES AND COSTA VERDE. BUT, SINCE YOU MENTION IT, I HAVE A PROPOSITION FOR YOU...
I'M SICK OF THIS BACKWATER COUNTRY, THIS DREARY PALACE, THAT FAT PIG ORTIZ AND HIS GANG OF TINPOT GENERALS. AND I HAVE ENOUGH MONEY TO LIVE IT UP ANYWHERE I CHOOSE.
WHERE ARE YOU GOING WITH THIS?
TO THIS: I HELP YOU GET OUT OF HERE AND LEAVE COSTA VERDE ALIVE. IN EXCHANGE, YOU TESTIFY IN MY FAVOUR TO CLEAR ME OF THE MURDERS OF JEREMY AND MATT ROWLAND AND ALLOW ME TO GO BACK TO THE U.S.A. WHAT DO YOU THINK?
I THINK YOU'RE EVEN MORE OF A BITCH THAN I REALISED.
AND YOU ARE STILL AS STUPID AS EVER. TOO BAD... YOU ASKED FOR IT...
CAPTAIN GARCIA! HELP!
?
41

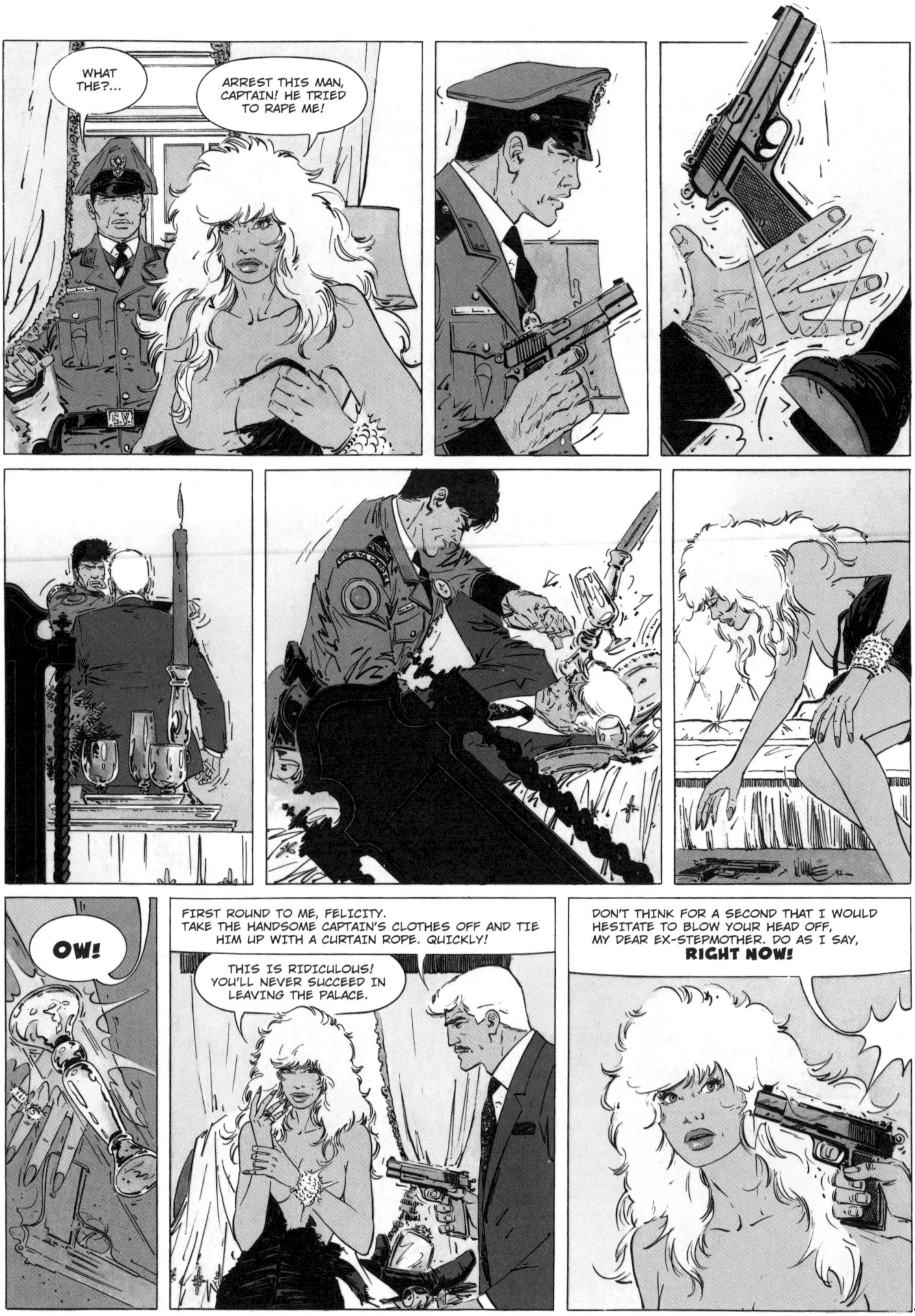
WHAT THE?...
ARREST THIS MAN, CAPTAIN! HE TRIED TO RAPE ME!
OW!
FIRST ROUND TO ME, FELICITY.
TAKE THE HANDSOME CAPTAIN'S CLOTHES OFF AND TIE HIM UP WITH A CURTAIN ROPE. QUICKLY!
THIS IS RIDICULOUS! YOU'LL NEVER SUCCEED IN LEAVING THE PALACE.
DON'T THINK FOR A SECOND THAT I WOULD HESITATE TO BLOW YOUR HEAD OFF, MY DEAR EX-STEPMOTHER. DO AS I SAY,
RIGHT NOW!
42

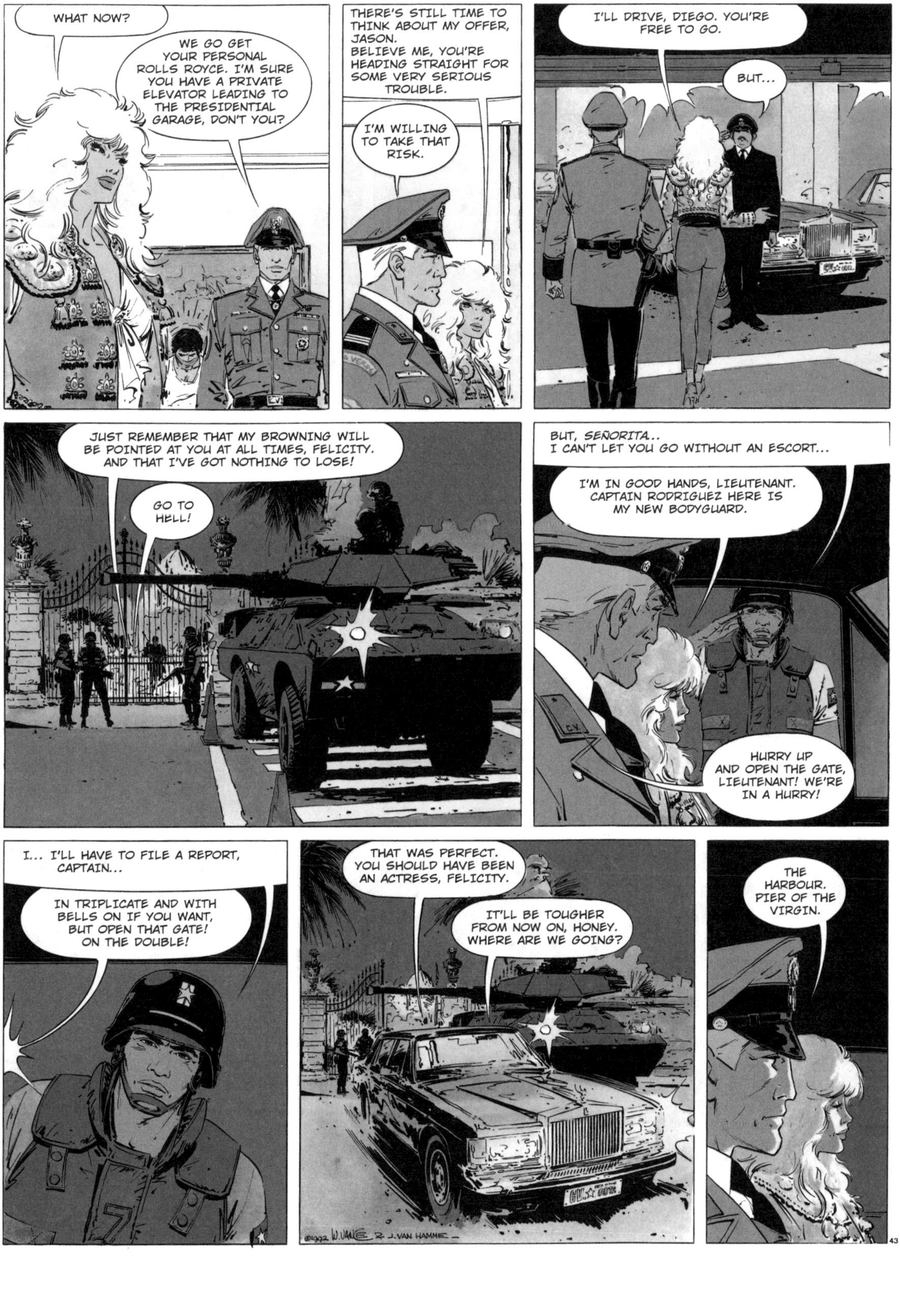
WHAT NOW?
WE GO GET YOUR PERSONAL ROLLS ROYCE. I'M SURE YOU HAVE A PRIVATE ELEVATOR LEADING TO THE PRESIDENTIAL GARAGE, DON'T YOU?
THERE'S STILL TIME TO THINK ABOUT MY OFFER, JASON. BELIEVE ME, YOU'RE HEADING STRAIGHT FOR SOME VERY SERIOUS TROUBLE.
I'M WILLING TO TAKE THAT RISK.
I'LL DRIVE, DIEGO. YOU'RE FREE TO GO.
BUT...
JUST REMEMBER THAT MY BROWNING WILL BE POINTED AT YOU AT ALL TIMES, FELICITY. AND THAT I'VE GOT NOTHING TO LOSE!
GO TO HELL!
BUT, SEÑORITA... I CAN'T LET YOU GO WITHOUT AN ESCORT...
I'M IN GOOD HANDS, LIEUTENANT. CAPTAIN RODRIGUEZ HERE IS MY NEW BODYGUARD.
HURRY UP AND OPEN THE GATE, LIEUTENANT! WE'RE IN A HURRY!
I... I'LL HAVE TO FILE A REPORT, CAPTAIN...
IN TRIPLICATE AND WITH BELLS ON IF YOU WANT, BUT OPEN THAT GATE! ON THE DOUBLE!
THAT WAS PERFECT. YOU SHOULD HAVE BEEN AN ACTRESS, FELICITY.
IT'LL BE TOUGHER FROM NOW ON, HONEY. WHERE ARE WE GOING?
THE HARBOUR. PIER OF THE VIRGIN.
©1992 W. VANCE & J. VAN HAMME
43

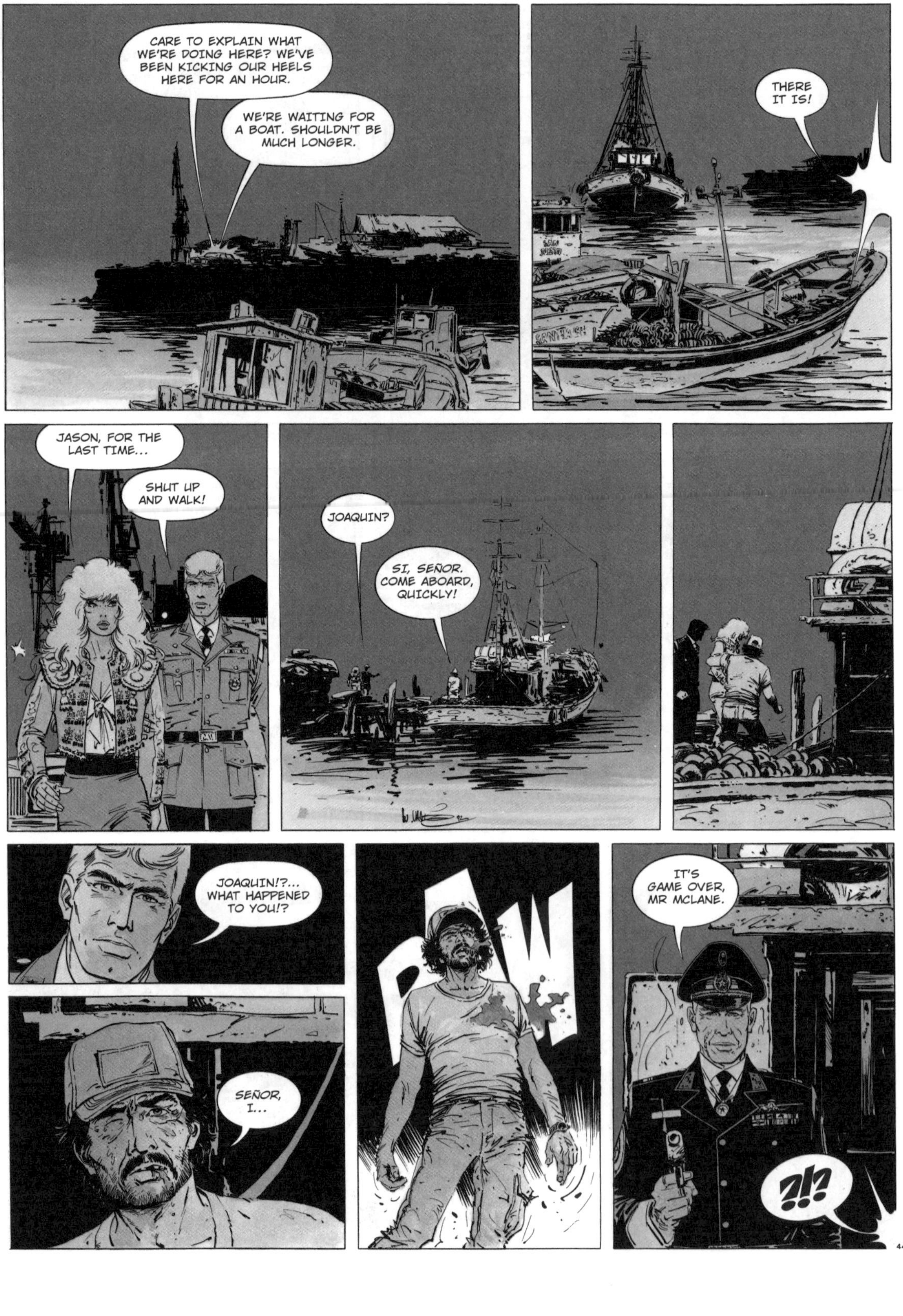
CARE TO EXPLAIN WHAT WE'RE DOING HERE? WE'VE BEEN KICKING OUR HEELS HERE FOR AN HOUR.
WE'RE WAITING FOR A BOAT. SHOULDN'T BE MUCH LONGER.
THERE IT IS!
JASON, FOR THE LAST TIME...
SHUT UP AND WALK!
JOAQUIN?
SI, SEÑOR. COME ABOARD, QUICKLY!
JOAQUIN!?... WHAT HAPPENED TO YOU!?
SEÑOR, I...
BAM
IT'S GAME OVER, MR MCLANE.
?!?
44

I TOLD YOU SO.

HA! HA! HA!

CLICK CLICK

YOU DIDN'T REALLY THINK THAT I'D LET YOU HAVE A LOADED WEAPON, SEÑOR?

GARCIA!? BUT, HOW?...

SIMPLE, MR MCLANE.

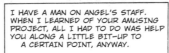

I HAVE A MAN ON ANGEL'S STAFF. WHEN I LEARNED OF YOUR AMUSING PROJECT, ALL I HAD TO DO WAS HELP YOU ALONG A LITTLE BIT—UP TO A CERTAIN POINT, ANYWAY.

YOU WERE PERFECT, QUERIDA. YOU WEREN'T TOO SCARED, WERE YOU?

ON THE CONTRARY. IT WAS VERY EXCITING. WHAT ARE WE GOING TO DO WITH HIM?

WE'LL TAKE HIM WHERE HE WANTED TO GO. YOU WANTED TO FIND MARIA DE LOS SANTOS, MR MCLANE? WELL, THEN, LET'S GO.

BLOP BLOP BLOP

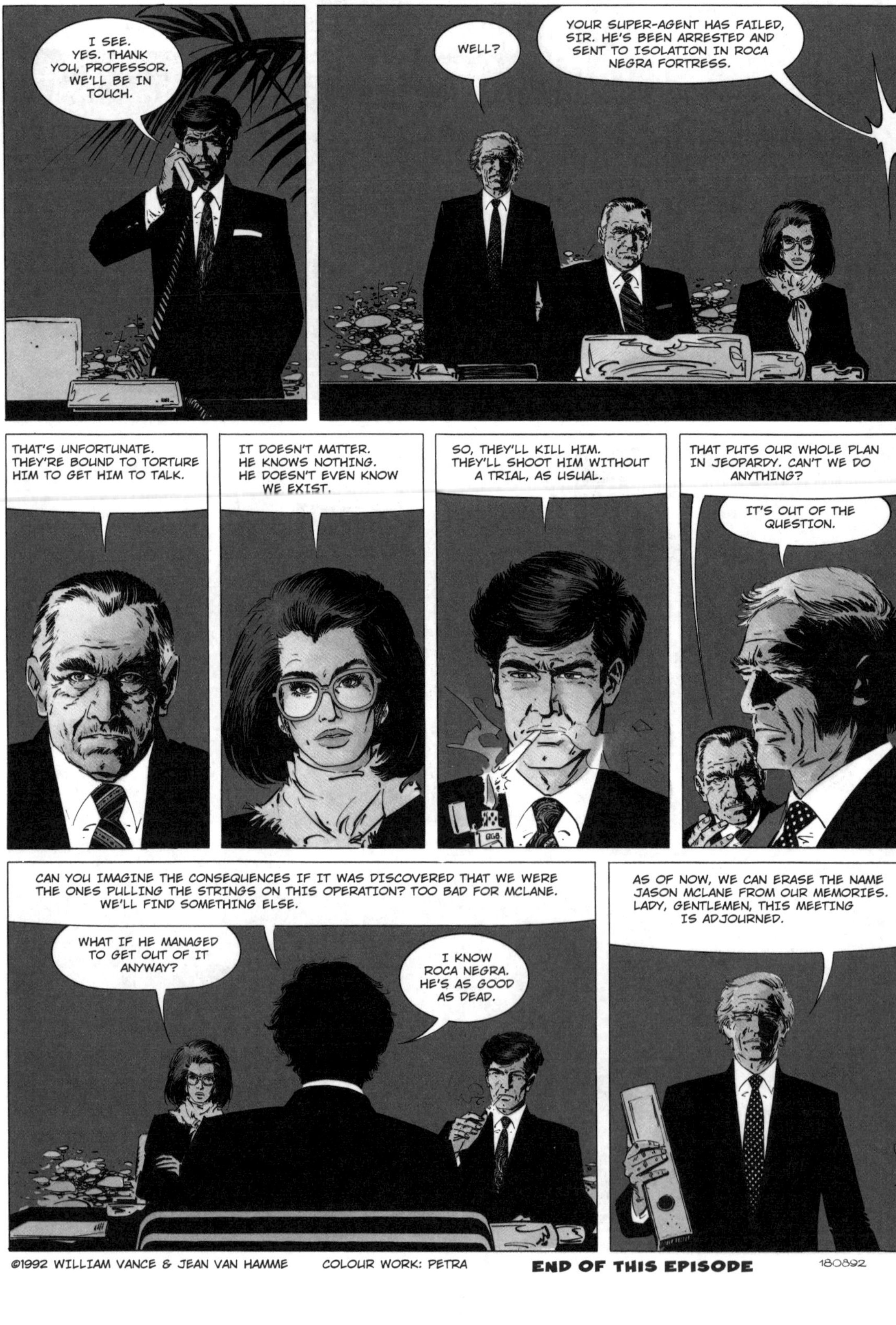

I SEE. YES. THANK YOU, PROFESSOR. WE'LL BE IN TOUCH.
WELL?
YOUR SUPER-AGENT HAS FAILED, SIR. HE'S BEEN ARRESTED AND SENT TO ISOLATION IN ROCA NEGRA FORTRESS.
THAT'S UNFORTUNATE. THEY'RE BOUND TO TORTURE HIM TO GET HIM TO TALK.
IT DOESN'T MATTER. HE KNOWS NOTHING. HE DOESN'T EVEN KNOW WE EXIST.
SO, THEY'LL KILL HIM. THEY'LL SHOOT HIM WITHOUT A TRIAL, AS USUAL.
THAT PUTS OUR WHOLE PLAN IN JEOPARDY. CAN'T WE DO ANYTHING?
IT'S OUT OF THE QUESTION.
CAN YOU IMAGINE THE CONSEQUENCES IF IT WAS DISCOVERED THAT WE WERE THE ONES PULLING THE STRINGS ON THIS OPERATION? TOO BAD FOR MCLANE. WE'LL FIND SOMETHING ELSE.
WHAT IF HE MANAGED TO GET OUT OF IT ANYWAY?
I KNOW ROCA NEGRA. HE'S AS GOOD AS DEAD.
AS OF NOW, WE CAN ERASE THE NAME JASON MCLANE FROM OUR MEMORIES. LADY, GENTLEMEN, THIS MEETING IS ADJOURNED.
46

 COLOUR WORK: PETRA **END OF THIS EPISODE** 180892